FEVER AND GUTS

A SYMPHONY

FEVER A SYMPHONY AND GUTS

JERRY D MATHES II

STEPHEN F. AUSTIN STATE UNIVERSITY PRESS
NACOGDOCHES ★ TEXAS

Stephen F. Austin State University Press
PO Box 13007, SFA Station,
Nacogcohes TX. 75962.
sfapress@sfasu.edu

Book Design by: Laura Davis
Cover Art: Charles Jones
Cover Design by: Laura Davis

"Hand-Me-Down War Stories," *That Mad Game: Growing Up in a Warzone: An Anthology of Essays from Around the Globe;* "The Lonely Bull," *The Sun;* "You Have a Beautiful Daughter," *Poigod Literary Magazine;* "Conception in a Time of Cold War," *Meadow;* "Hand-Me Down War Stories," *The Southern Review;* "Ahead of the Flaming Front," *High Desert Journal;* "Striking into Nothingness," *Baltimore Review.* This essay was also included in the anthology, *Borne on Air.* Eastern Washington University Press; "Moving in Gangland," *Talking River;* "Sex and the Single Swimming Pool," originally titled, "For the First Time: Desert Pool," *Smyles and Fish;* "An Absence of Motion," *Mid-American Review;* "American Losers," *Rebel 47.*

ISBN: 978-1-936205-85-1

First Edition

Acknowledgments

I want to extend my gratitude to Kimberly Verhines at SFASU Press who saw enough value in my essays to invest time and effort into the production of this book. Also thanks to those others involved with the production, Laura McKinney, Brittany O'Sullivan, and Laura Davis. You all are awesome. The road to this book was long, and I would be remiss if I didn't acknowledge my first nonfiction teacher, Mark Sanders, who read some of these essays in their first draft. I need to thank those that followed: Claire Davis, Kim Barnes, Alex Albright, Mary Clearman Blew, and all of the living and dead writers whose words inspired and taught me from the page. I appreciate my fellow students of writing and impromptu writing groups over the years: Ida, Dean, Ryan A., AnnE, Lucas, Kelly, Andrea, Matt, Lisa, Kim, Annie, Mike, Ryan F., Linda, and the others. A special thanks to The Southernmost Writers' Workshop in the World at South Pole Station and Andre Fleuette, Kate Macfarlane Javes, and Paddy Douglas who inspired me with their work. I must also mention the Jack Kent Cooke Foundation and the scholarship they saw fit to award me, making it possible for me to study writing at the University of Idaho. Grad school would never have been possible without their support.

CONTENTS

As always, for the Girl Posse.

FEVER AND GUTS: A SYMPHONY

I

In the store by the bath towels, the fever comes. Right between the lamps and household appliances, the nausea begins. It stirs the gut like low heat under a pot of soup. The car seems so far away, out in the far end of the lot because you like to walk and now, in the swirling mass of shoppers on a Monday night, it feels as good as across Texas, across the rolling hills thickened with pines, down into the waterless expanses of dead canyons filled with dry wind and over the oil-stained sea. The car, an oasis of transport. You talk on the cell phone with your last-wife as you dodge between the cars' headlights. She had been telling you about her day, the bitch at work who just doesn't get it, how hard the Idaho winter ended and your grade-school daughters' day, one has clarinet recital coming fast and the other wants to be in chess club-oh they need canvas and paint. She urges you to go rest, but go by the pharmacy first, get some medicine. But you're not listening. You don't feel like going into another store, standing in line, and waiting while people jostle around crowding you. You can handle this. Soon it will be a bad memory. The fever makes you want a drink of water more than a beer. When did this happen? You drive, not sure if the shaking in the steering wheel is in the tires or your bones.

Home, sitting at the desk, believing it's not going to get worse. Dizzy, your vision blurs and the words squirm like mashed gnats in the book you try to read. You wish you could throw up or crap, but the pressure is trapped in your gut and pushes outward like an expanding puffer fish trapped in the torso's muscle and bone. The text: *How are you?* Your ex-girlfriend is extremely grammatical in her texts and proud of her Minnesota public education. *Think I'm sick* The bed, lie down. From upright walking to laid out like a victim in less than ten minutes. *Sorry⊗* You swim. The air wavers in the room, undersea currents like when you went overboard in the Bering Sea and you looked down toward the depths to see your feet, terrified your boots would suck you to the bottom. You struggled to pull them off and they slipped away into the current, wavering, wavering, wavering. It is not the sea you swim against and you don't shiver from Arctic currents, it is the sweat and spasm of fever.

These shattered kaleidoscopic memories, fractured and out of sequence, but of peculiar order. What's this mystery of association? Meditation. A blonde ex-wife, a

Korean linguist turned black jack dealer with a blond son conceived in Korea by a Ukrainian. An ex-stepson you wonder about because you became attached and detached at the whims of adults. How fast the move from stepfather to ex-father, sign the paper and you're done. He'll only know you as a 31 year-old man. At the time you never want to be a stepdad again. Why them, why now? No the blonde ex-wife married in Vegas half asleep with drinking at mid-morning. She wore a sundress and you an army field jacket, the first time and you weren't even twenty. No children, nor nieces nor nephews, we were all alone to crash against the shores of each other's bodies. No the half-Mexican/half-Irish woman you married in a forested wildfire-camp in the mountains, the mother of your children. The two daughters you talked to before the sudden onset of illness, the youngest with copper colored hair who at eight already has a woman's smile and always asks if you've seen any animals today and the oldest a decade old with a sand shimmered mane and pensive brown eyes who always asks when will you be back. Grade-school girls who ride the bus each day and look out on empty streets where other parents stand. Before, before, and before. Dad, we miss you. That's the oldest. The youngest calls you Papa and wants to know why boys have to be asses. They both tell you to quit saying, "fuck." They weary of the jobs that keep you at a distance, Dad get something closer. Why all the wildfires? Why the South Pole? Why Texas? They understand the ritual of sacrifice. You shouldn't have had the tacos for dinner.

Hand-Me-Down
War Stories

Wars don't only affect those who fight them, wars go on for generations.

Tim O'Brien

1991: Goodsprings, Nevada

I was twenty-six, sitting in my parents' kitchen. Photos hung across from where my mother's spoon collection tarnished on the wall. They lived in another isolated part of the West, the southern Nevada desert where he was a foreman at a power plant across the California state line. I lived in Las Vegas where I worked as a night auditor in a hotel / casino and had been thinking about war. The American military was massing in the Saudi region of the Arabian Desert and the Persian Gulf for the first time. As a former armor crewman, I knew I might get called up if things didn't go well. My father was sitting in the living room, reading a crime novel with the television on, which he had done for as long as I could remember. He closed the book, walked in, and lit a cigarette. He sat across from me. Smoke drifted around him, and he said, "One night we were hit hard. NVA regulars and Cong sappers slithered into the wire. Mortar rounds blew our Hueys off the pads." I felt obligated to listen. My mother was visiting my sister. My father and I were alone in a quiet house.

"Me and West Virginia grabbed our sixteens and fired for all we had. It looked like a million North Vietnamese under the flares. Squiggling and squirming. Even though you knew every time bullets started you could get hit, this was one of those times I put my chips on us all dying."

My eyes drifted to the photos on the wall behind him: my mom at sixteen in a bikini, my mom holding me as an infant, my mom holding each of her other four children, groups of us, and a professionally taken family portrait.

"We lowered artillery and fired into them. Kept them back for hours. High explosive rounds, bunker busters, and Willie Peter—that white phosphorous is some nasty shit. The jungle burned. We saw rows and rows of shadows flailing around in the bush, climbing over each other. They screamed. Some sappers got through the wire and one got into our bunker. I turned, pushed the barrel into his chest, and fired. A full burst stitched his ass up the center. It was all fucked up. Blood and bone everywhere, bullets and casings, West Virginia screaming his ass off, and even more fucked up—I liked it." He placed his cigarette in the ashtray. "You want a beer?"

I nodded, and as he left, I thought of the campfire in

Arizona where we had lived in tents when I was twelve. His desert-stained Stetson shifted back on his head as he laughed so loud I thought the coyotes would return his call. He chased gold like salvation and stayed faithful to his wife and kids with the persistence of the war, while struggling against the common life. We lived in the twentieth-century frontier, believing the myth that it was still possible to stake out a piece of ground and make something out of the land. During those desert years, he looked for a place to hold on to and hammered a boy in cutoffs into a disjointed man whose life had been defined by hardship and suffering.

My father handed me a bottle of beer and sat down. Gray haired and fat in the belly, he still had a strength that surprised me, stronger than most the guys my age. His cigarette smoldered in the ashtray. Behind him, amid those other photos, my mother's wedding photo taken when he was eighteen, a year and ten months before he went to Vietnam.

MAY 1983: FORT KNOX, KENTUCKY

I turned nineteen in basic training. The drill sergeants marched us privates—or "dicks," as they called us—into gas chambers and turned us into crying, choking, vomiting children. We entered the cinder-block buildings with our protective masks on and were ordered to remove them. It was like taking a punch in the solar plexus while inhaling gasoline. Beforehand, they instructed us to exit the chamber and walk, flapping our arms in a slow rhythmic fashion to shake off any of the CS tear gas. Aside from sloughing off the gas, the action, I believe, gave us something to focus on to control our panic. As I waited my turn, the first recruits lurched from the chamber. Drill sergeants were clucking and yelling, "Don't run, chicken-boy. Flap them wings, private. You're flapping too fast, dick; are you flagging down a trick to fuck?" Some of us dropped to our knees like drunks. "Get up—move, dick—I didn't give you permission to stop. Rubbing your eyes makes it worse, idiot." The gas burned our skin, stabbed our eyes shut, and scorched our lungs as if we were breathing in raw flame. Some ran blind through the Kentucky woods, flapping, streaming tears, and screaming like camouflaged birds struggling to gain airspeed, colliding into trees or tumbling off embankments, mixing blood and tear gas. I did not want to be the guy who dropped to his knees—a quitter or the guy who ran—the unnerved.

I heard my father's voice, "You pussy, stand up, this ain't shit," like when we played touch football as kids and he'd stiff-arm my eighty-pound body to the ground. "Stand up and figure out how to get around my arm. You quit, you die." I walked and flapped and took the gas. I stood and took the shouting, I took the push-ups, the squat thrusts, the sit-ups, the marching, and the running. I took the pain because, like the gas chamber, there was no escaping it.

I won the George S. Patton Jr. Award for being honor graduate at Fort Knox, and now I related to my father as a military man: the awe of tracers at night like a string of Christmas lights, the distant storm of artillery in the far mountains, the acceleration of life when the big guns stop your pulse, and the Gatling guns' ripsaw sound from ground attack aircraft. We shared drill instructors, bad food, dirt, and munitions, but "least you ain't facing the Nam."

My generation of soldiers fought the end of the Cold

War, training to fight in Germany against the Soviet Bloc, while other smaller conflicts went on: peace-keeping missions, the invasion of Grenada, and the invasion of Panama. It seemed then that the massed weight of armored divisions would never see battle unless the Warsaw Pact gambled that they had more to gain than lose by attacking Western Europe. Rabid to face fire and prove ourselves, many of the soldiers hoped the enemy so foolish. We also learned to see our enemy as subhuman, and at the same time, gave them respect for being worthy opponents. A strange contradiction, but one I heard many times from my father.

In basic training, the army issued me a set of dog tags. We privates gave the essential facts: blood type, Social Security number that doubles as a service number, name, and the only piece of information a recruit could choose—religious preference. I told the clerk "agnostic," but he said that means no religious preference, which, stamped on the tin tag reads: no rel pref. Our enemy was the Soviet Union, the Russian Communists who had abolished religion. Therefore, telling the army you lacked faith was to sympathize with the enemy. "Only faggots and Commies deny God," a drill sergeant yelled.

The drill sergeants also informed us that the Godless do not survive on the battlefield. "Kill Russians! Shoot to kill, kill for thrill!" they yelled. "Only the faithful face fire and continue forward."

My father mocked such platitudes. "God loves you so he's going to splatter your friend's guts all over you and make you lie in your own shit for a couple of days." I had grown used to hearing him say things like, "The Lord is my shepherd leading me to slaughter," and "turn the other cheek, love thy neighbor, but burn down his hut, drop a grenade in his well, and shoot his water buffalo first." Once, after Sunday school when everyone gathered to chat before regular services, a woman said to my father that God must have looked after him to bring him home alive. My father took a drag from his cigarette and told her God must've been looking the other way when his buddies were killed.

My father told us: "A guy I went to school with was coming home. He had done his year in the shit and caught that freedom bird home to Cincinnati. His family went to meet him at the airport. They got their signs, Welcome Home, Daddy. Love You, Son. They got their little flags and balloons. You just know they had their faces pressed to glass picking out planes. "It's that one, no that one. Is it landing?" My father took a concentrated drag from his Raleigh. "That airliner busted a hillside," his voice as flat as a town leveled by artillery.

As I stood in line for my dog tags, I thought about being in sixth grade, and my father giving me Bertrand Russell's, *Why I Am Not a Christian*. I had seen him reading the book in his recliner, fogged in by cigarette smoke and bursts of laughter. "You need more than that book of fairy tales to live by. Any moron can hold a book of myth and claim absolute authority. No one to prove them wrong. It takes a strong person to use logic and reason." I had quit going to church by this time. I couldn't make the connection to the science I learned and the philosophy my father used to argue against any faith. He told me warriors were killers and killers could never enter the Promised Land, regardless of what the preachers said. When I expressed my doubt to church friends they said I'd burn in hell. My father scoffed, "There is no hell."

My father said, "They should get themselves a killer's religion they like to war so much." Maybe they had. And when the soldier standing behind the counter asked me again if I was sure about religious preference, I told him, "No doubt in my mind, sir."

1979: IRON CREEK, ARIZONA

My uncle Larry owned a cabin outside of Prescott, Arizona, near a church camp where my mother had spent her childhood summers. We lived there the last part of the spring of my eighth-grade year and a month into the summer before ninth grade as my father finished working at a sawmill before heading to a truck-driving job in the iron mine at Eagle Mountain, California. We never attended religious services. Little more than one room, the cabin was anchored onto a steep mountainside. A deck ran the entire front and had milk urns with tractor seats welded on top. Only my parents and sister slept in the cabin; we boys slept on the forest ground and huddled around ponderosa pines when it rained. A creek cut through the forest and hugged a cliff that we climbed, never realizing we were one missed handhold away from dying. In the evening, the sun disappeared behind high, tree-fringed ridges and kept a pale light hovering above the canyons. When the canyons darkened, we gathered in the cabin and ate, and after homework, played cards or my father read us *The Lord of the Rings*. The lanterns in the cabin shone out from curtainless windows, and when I returned late from hikes, the panes were like lighthouse mirrors.

My father would begin a story when no one expected it. Four of us were playing Hearts at the cabin's dining table; my father placed his hand face-down on the table. "Them marines were pissed. They found a bunch of POWs in some gook hospital bunker, strapped down with their balls cut off. Some guys even had bamboo slivers shoved down their dicks. The marines captured these Viet Cong nurses and doctors, and we were flying in to pull everyone out." His hands mimicked the helicopters' rapid descent into the landing zone. "The LZ was clear, and these marines were busy working out their rage. These guys had taken a shit load of KIAs and finding their buddies mutilated made them nuts." He reached into his sock and pulled a pack of Raleighs. Casual.

"I'm not shitting. These jarheads popped a flare up an NVA nurse's twat." He slammed his free palm into the pack's bottom as if firing the flare. "Smoke rolled up into the rotor wash and down through the bird. You smell a body burn, you don't forget it." He scooped up his cards and passed left.

The stories related war as the province of honorable men performing at the edge of human limits. Atrocities are only men surviving unfathomable conditions. Those marines and aircrews would go home and love their families and live as if in a separate life. Some men's minds would snap and become their own enemy. But it was the war as a whole, and how it was revealed in the stories, that meant I would never understand the two-way mirror between the civilized, caring human being and the savage killer on the battlefield.

1976: SOUTHERN ARIZONA DESERT

The stories didn't exist at first: aphorisms, examples, and imperatives. "A man who can't sit still, dies," my father told me. "You see a straight line, a man put it there. Nature doesn't work with a straight edge." By the sixth grade, I learned that with a knife and a coil of parachute cord a man could survive in any environment, and without these two vital supplies, poor substitutes could be manufactured.

My father said the "Spartans started as children," hardening themselves in the environment and learning to be resourceful, before learning anything of war. I spent hours lying in the desert, watching tortoises crossing yards away, letting lizards run over my back, and picking out distant roads and abandoned cars, mining shafts and shacks, fantasizing of being loose in the Lacedaemonian countryside in only a cloak, acclimatizing myself to hardship.

By the middle of my seventh-grade year, my family of six lived in tents in the Arizona desert, close to the Mexico-New Mexico border. After my father gave up his small-town judgeship in Gilbert, Arizona, he and my mother decided to make a life like homesteaders—pioneers pushing the edges of an illusory frontier. He hoped the Yankees wouldn't move out west and ruin this place like they had Dixie. My parents owned a mortgage on forty acres and planned to build a house out of creek rocks, adobe, and our sweat. This was where he told us about Cochise and his stronghold in the Dragoon Mountains that towered over the desert like a medieval fortress, northwest of our land. How Cochise had fought the army to a standstill for eleven years. U.S. forces captured the Chiricahua Apache in 1871, but he escaped before the army could ship him to a reservation, and fought until the next year when, with the help of an Anglo friend, he negotiated the terms of his surrender. Part of the terms was that he would not be forced out of Arizona to Florida or Oklahoma, but would remain an exile in his own land. My father loved the story of how the small, native force held the Union Army back for eleven years before losing with grace. He loved their bravery most of all.

Aside from the few cowboys riding through, we saw no one. My two brothers were three and four years younger than I was, and my sister seven years younger. We boys tracked each other across the expanse of yucca plants, cacti, mesquite bushes, and stunted trees. Dry washes crosshatched the land and small arroyos ran out of distant mountains to the east that rose off the desert floor like a giant city skyline. One of us would take off with up to an hour's head start. Blond, barefoot, and wearing cutoffs, we created false trails, tried to obliterate our tracks and hid as close to the trail as possible so that we could stand up when the others passed by and say, "You're dead."

We sat under a sunset the color of cracked-open pomegranates and smeared grapes. Our campfire was the only light for miles. A cast-iron pot of pinto beans simmered. My father shined a handheld spotlight beyond our ring of fire, and we saw hundreds of eyes staring. "Rabbits" my father said. Coyotes yipped and howled in the foothills, and the purple orbs floated in the black, like a meteor belt between the deep desert and us.

We six squatted on rocks, feral in firelight. "No amount of fear's going to keep them jackrabbits alive any longer." He looked out into the desert. "We had this communications sergeant who was really scared. Sure, everyone walked around like the next step would blow their balls off, but this guy was tripped out. He lined his cot with flak vests and slept under the hot pieces of shit. We all slept in the bunker, but he thought it wasn't safe enough." My father added some mesquite to the fire and stirred it around; it flared and cracked. My mother checked the beans.

My father drank from his coffee mug. "Now the Cong used to drop a couple of mortar rounds or shoot a rocket into the perimeter at night. Only enough to fuck with us and make sure we didn't sleep all night. It got to be that we wouldn't roll off the racks until the fifth round because the odds of a ground assault went up. Harassment fire was usually only a couple rounds.

"But one night, a round hit close and dumped us all on our asses. Some guys scrambled around, some of us hugged the floor for a second and went for our sixteens, but that commo guy stayed on his bunk, under the weight of those flak jackets. Them gooks were only probing us. It wasn't more than ten minutes before we were back smoking, wondering if they were going to hit again. That fucker still lying on his cot." My father held up a thorn from a mesquite branch. "A piece of shrapnel no bigger than this nailed him in the head. A sliver of steel—God must've really wanted him dead." He flicked the thorn into the fire as the coyotes howled.

1975: Gilbert, Arizona

My father combed the deserts for gold. He dragged me through Mogollon Rim country, the Hassayampa River, and Oak Creek Canyon looking for flakes and nuggets in pans and sluice boxes. But in the Superstition Mountains we started looking for a different kind of gold, lost gold from Spanish conquistadors who'd searched for the Seven Cities of Gold, Cíbola and Quivira (El Dorado), de Vaca's legend and the secret markings, like Catholic hieroglyphs, of Monks Fray Marcos and Marcos de Niza, that revealed trails leading to riches: gold crosses, goblets, chains, rings, bracelets, coins, idols, utensils, plates, and ingots molded in ancient gold smithies—and not just gold, but also gems encrusting the artifacts. Portuguese bishops fleeing their lost war with the Moors had fled west across the Atlantic with sacred treasures and, somehow, hid the treasure in the Superstitions. Don Miguel Peralta found a gold vein on the northern edge of his Church Grant lands. The Apaches said the Thunder God had put the gold in the mountains for the tribe to use only in times of need, and massacred the Peralta family.

In the nineteenth century, Jacob "The Dutchman" Walz's Apache wife would lead him to the gold mine, and her tribe killed her for revealing the secret. Some twisted arroyo is hidden by the Lost Dutchman Mine, and enough gold dust has turned up on burros wandering ownerless out of the wilderness to keep people thinking the mine is still out there, cursed. Rumors of maps and hoaxes of stones showing the way filled the legend, but when Walz died in 1891, no one knew for certain where the mine was.

My father often said, "The desert's so full of legends, something's bound to be out there."

The legends bloomed like cactus blossoms, bright and fleeting in a dry land. We gave up dry panning dead streams, the sluicing of running creeks, and started hiking miles of ridgelines and ravines. The crucial details were Needle Canyon, Weaver's Needle, and a natural arch. My father and his partner, Tom, both carried packs, revolvers and twelve-gauge shotguns. I wore an old, USMC pack on my back containing a folding knife that had several blades, cans of Vienna sausage, bread, and survival equipment. I carried a pump-action BB gun because I was eleven. My father said the guns were for snakes and pumas, but I realized he was leading me on combat patrols across a scarred desert.

We hiked just below ridgelines so as not to skyline ourselves, laid up in brush or behind rock cairns for breaks, looked for tracks and signs of people in the trails, and methodically scouted the terrain ahead and behind for human movement—claim jumpers. I thought it was part of my training—my becoming a warrior, not my being a warrior: the watching of shadows, avoiding others in the woods or deserts, looking at signs in the brush and dirt that would tell me of their passing.

My father and Tom met another man who had a small claim and turned out to be a liar. He said he had a map to the Lost Dutchman's Mine or at least a strike so rich they'd never work again. He needed help because he was too broke and too old to get it by himself. It would be a hard hike up into the highest part of the Superstitions and they decided to get mules and lay up provisions for an extended foray. When the two mules appeared in our suburban backyard, my brothers and I were the coolest kids around.

My father worked as a cop then, right before he became a judge. One night he came home early, and all I knew was something had gone wrong. The partner living out at his claim placed an emergency call: someone had bushwhacked him, and he needed help. My father changed his uniform for his Stetson, jeans, shirt, and cowboy boots, but kept the gun belt, carrying his .357 revolver. He loomed over us, and when he pointed at me to mind my mother, his finger looked like a nightstick. Mother packed him some food and kissed him at the door as if he were leaving for work. This is what men do: go to the aid of their partners, or others in need, even strapping on their guns to do so. The call turned out to be a false alarm and by the time summer was over, my father abandoned going into the Superstitions.

It was during this time I realized that I lived among war's flotsam: fatigues, dress blues, rank and unit patches, ribbons, brass insignia, medals that he hung on a plaque. Bullet casings I tasted on my hands long after my mother forced me to wash before dinner. A dud mortar round (which I took to my third-grade class for show-and-tell), and a boonie hat kept in a box from a shredded friend. Some sacred relics I showed my friends and pretended to know the meaning of what stories these things told.

1973: GILBERT, ARIZONA

Around the time I was in the fourth grade, the first POWs came home from Vietnam, the U.S. forces pulled back to their Cold War bases, and I began to realize my father was a veteran. I had always known it, but it was in the way I knew he worked at the foundry and that they both involved steel and heat. And this was the same year I started to discover that in my father's household surviving was not the only virtue. Did I suffer well? I battered myself regardless of odds or handicaps, or the agon. I learned, as the Spartans knew, suffering made you strong.

"What do you mean you ran away?" My father's frame

filled the doorway.

"They were three, big high schoolers and my ankle hurt."

"In the jungle, Charlie's not going to let you call a fucking time-out because you got a sore ankle. And he's bringing more than three, big high schoolers. I've told you, you're either the wolf or the sheep. Which fucking is it, boy, wolf or sheep?" He shut the door. I held my books on the mown lawn, waiting for a beating. It would not be the last time I stood in front of a group of bullies bigger than I, but it was the last time I sought refuge from my father.

1966: GLENDALE, ARIZONA

My earliest memory is of a parade for my father returning from the war. Bright, streaming sun squeezed through tree branches, backlighting the leaves as if the chlorophyll made them glow. My father, his blue uniform heavy with medals, shook hands with people on the street as convertibles drove by between groups of horses and marching bands. A balloon hovered above, clear with a powder blue Mickey Mouse head inside. It tugged against the string as it bobbed away. My mother smiled in a way I would never see her do again, her long, blond hair reaching almost to her miniskirt, and gripped my father in a way that felt good to me. I was happy. Everyone was waving, smiling, laughing, and shaking hands, hugging in the summer warmth of a parade, a homecoming for men deployed in the first call-up to Vietnam.

All through my childhood this memory cropped up and caught me wanting my own homecoming. My father spoke of the Confederacy and the veterans who were left with nothing but a run for the Texas plains and hill country—a home taken by the enemy bankers and agents. I counted the years between our wars—from the Revolution on—and calculated the probability of seeing action in my youth. Films, television, and books supplemented my father's stories. The tragedy was glorified, but even then I bought into the point of view of war. Narrators always lived. Even if the protagonist died on the battlefield, the narrator went on, and I saw myself as the storyteller, the omniscient and truest survivor.

The films and books that filled my life were *The Sands of Iwo Jima, Patton, Apocalypse Now, Battle of the Bulge, Guadalcanal Diary, The Iliad, A Farewell to Arms, A Bridge Too Far, If I Die in a Combat Zone, Fire in the Lake, The Short Timers, Body Count,* and *A Rumor of War.* I filled my mind with military traditions and history from grade school through high school, from Ash Creek, Peoria, Prescott, Skull Valley, Eagle Mountain, and Baker, California. I read Che Guevara's book, memorized the names of all the terrorist and guerilla organizations, and could just about identify every weapon in use by militaries all over the world. I had sat in rural libraries across the southwest flipping through Jane's Infantry Weapons, imagining each weapon's weight in my hands.

1965: GLENDALE, ARIZONA

My Kentuckian father received orders for deployment to Vietnam as a nineteen-year-old, helicopter door gunner. He idolized James Dean and tough-guy actors like Robert Mitchum and John Wayne and loved the novels of Louis L'Amour, Zane Grey, and Robert Heinlein. Just a couple years before, he was coaching his brother's junior-high football team and racing old cars on back roads, missing the postwar boom of the fifties because his parents drank away all the family's money. He never had a television in his house, but listened to Elvis and Jimmy Horton on the radio. He was an all-state athlete and dropped out of school and joined the air force to get away. The word Vietnam probably never entered his hillbilly world, but he would witness a new lexicon arise from that country.

In a black-and-white photo, he crouches on a beach in the Philippines right before flying to DaNang. Slim and athletic, he only wears shorts, and even in the colorless photo, his tan is apparent. Later that year, over a besieged firebase called Pleiku, a rocket will hit his gunship, and it will crash onto the edge of an airstrip, and he will sprint over open ground to negotiate the wire, and vault over the barricade into the siege—the sole crew member to survive. Before the year's end, hit with heavy machine-gun fire, a second ship will pile into the jungle a long way from any firebase. The crew chief, blown against the bulkhead, will be alive, but unconscious. My wounded father will extract himself from the wreckage and carry the first-aid kit, an M16, and the crew chief to safety, evading the enemy for days, while living on bad water and folded photographs.

After surviving the war, he isolated and besieged himself and his family in the deserts and forests of the west. We fled one place after another, surviving by the slightest edge at times, but surviving. I have often wondered who the young man was in the photo on the beach or the groom in his uniform before he learned the language of war. During his tour he was on five helicopters that were shot down. Everyone in his original crew was killed, as well as everyone in his second crew. He became intimate with suffering. He wrote letters to my mother, and I am told that before flying out on missions, he looked at his family's pictures and kissed them as if they were religious icons. All these things before he turned twenty, before I turned two, with the stories knotting inside him, waiting to shape us both.

An Absence of Motion

The neurologist says every kid gets one seizure, but after that, we should worry. Funny, I thought; I had a skipper in Alaska say, "Everyone should survive one big storm—after that a person ought to be worried the weather is out to get them." And this from a guy who hummed or sang Gordon Lightfoot's, "The Wreck of the Edmund Fitzgerald," every day.

"Where does the love of a good God go, when the waves turn the minutes to hours?"

Storms are motion. Violent storms are extreme motion that can tear away earth and water. Tornados plow suburbs into fields, hurricanes flood so far inland that people believe a second Deluge has come, thunderstorms build up and create winds snapping off trees and housetops bringing rain, flash floods, eroding towns to silt. Lightning ionizes the air, driving atoms to electrified frenzy, killing more people a year than any other phenomena. Weather's harshest moment is an absence of motion, more destructive and insidious than the cinema-graphic drama of storms.

The center of a hurricane is quiet.

Seizures are the high pressure of illness, the horse latitudes, and fighting a seizure is like trying to stop the weather, pointless and fearsome. The substrate of consciousness squeezed until nothing happens. My two-year-old daughter's nerves, roots of her motion, quit. I didn't see it start; Kathy, my wife, did. I saw it midway through and the aftermath. Sophia looked like what I expected electrocution victims to look like, color fried from her skin, drool, fluttering whites of eyes and a head lolling on a grounded-out neck.

Winds aloft have no distinct separation from surface winds.

For all the sea storms that cracked ships in half, the doldrums clenched ships until the crew cracked. Think of the herds of horses floating bloated, stranded between Cancer and Capricorn, not grazing the Sargasso Sea. Driven overboard for lack of water, hooves churning chaotic currents, the ocean had not seen such movement for weeks, until the last chuff, flared nostrils sucking slack water—kicking for the bottom, riderless, believing they can make landfall. Sailors gazed at a tattered horizon, wanting wind more than water. Salt flats. All that brine and urine, hardtack and weevils and visions of fruit on a far shore that lookouts in the crow's nest thought they could sometimes see. Laughter creaked like the ship's tortured timbers shrinking above the waterline. The tropical sun does not hang high; it bears down, forcing leviathans to break the surface, the silence.

A whirlpool is water collapsing in on itself.

My daughter had a small fever, and the neurologist reassures us, a temperature spike could trigger a seizure—a febrile fever. It can happen to any normal kid. For all I know, this is unheard of in my family, but later my mother will tell me that I, and my sister, had them. Doesn't anybody believe in sharing the info? Of course, Mom thinks I should have asked a long time ago, like asking for a forecast. I wonder if she has other observations I need to predict the future.

A meteorologist can spot a tropical depression coming, but can't stop it. The defining mark of a tropical depression: closed off circulation.

High-pressure summer systems press down an area, exerting force so air flows nowhere, stales, and locks dust and smoke in the sky— rust on the side of a stock tank. The air poisons and starts killing, and in the summer, it heats and thickens like a sheepherder's stew. Drought for the want of thunder. Desiccated livestock and cracked clay and even the cacti turn brown and relinquish pulp to dust.

When cold, air masses sink.

The neurologist also says, traveling on a long trip, such as we did, with the accompanying bad diet of fast food and general road wear can bring on a seizure, especially with the radical temperature fluctuations of late fall days and the warmth of the truck. The temperature switch shocks the fatigued body and road-numbed mind.

Thermal belts are trapped warmth, surrounded by colder air, calmed mid-slope.

The Santa Ana and Chinook are foehn winds, reversing normal air currents and inflicting havoc after forcing the sky to stand still. After the switch, wildfire fighters can find their safe areas overrun with flames.

Lightning doesn't always find the earth.

In winter, the hard frost of a clear high night drives sap into root tips, freezing the air to branches. Sun ice-blinds and heat dissipates into the air and you cannot stop it, no matter how hard you flail your arms. Warmth must always bleed itself into the cold. The motionless sky grows quiet, and you can hear the ice freeze. Hear the coldest water rise and solidify the surface. The winter high will coerce snowshoe hares into hiding for fear of freezing, until a storm ushers warmth ahead of the low. Cirrus clouds, mares tails of ice, lower to nimbus—comforters for the sky.

Virga is rain that doesn't touch the earth.

The experience of my daughter's seizure was like when I almost drowned in the Bering Sea. For all I had, for all I knew, no amount of fighting will save or change a damn thing. The distant shore ignores the sea, a bored god, voiceless and silent.

The calm is the warning.

Helplessness in a time of binding. High Pressure is a stable atmosphere—involuntary indecision, motionless as gulfs of low-pressure whirl all around. Jagged edges of isobars. A seizure, rigid—fighting the weather is waiting for motion on its own accord. I learned these things about weather as early as the Boy Scout Manual's description of clouds, as early as my father looking into the Southwest sky and saying, "It's going to be dry a while."

Horizontal eddies are cyclones rolling sideways.

The neurologist says we'll have to watch her. The EKG says all the wiring's fine, no organic anomalies. The phrase "organic anomaly" makes me cringe, like when I knew I couldn't out swim the riptide. A slow smolder in gut, like the sun's rays through a magnifying glass.

Meteorologists can be wrong—a lot—and keep their jobs, but they do save lives.

The center of a tornado is calm and green.

The neurologist says we have to watch her for signs: mixed hot and cold on fatiguing drives, a drought of juice, too many snacks, or watch her for gazing off, eyes folding into her skull, stiff limbs quivering like lightning moving cloud to cloud, out of reach, impotent. Daydreaming, tired, or seized and frozen waiting for me to help her, touch her, and tell her the bad weather will pass.

American Losers

OLE! and surged, my feet had never known such swiftness, thinking my legs couldn't pump any faster and it was a dream where I buck a wind, going nowhere, full speed. The sangría, drunk in luscious sips before I stood astride cobblestones, roiled my gut and drained lead into my feet—bulls don't care about spendy running shoes, only my ass and their horns. The village, *Arcos de la Frontera*, erected on a cliff's edge that drops into a chasm thousands of feet, down thousands of years before *El Cid* and *Don Quixote*, and sunflowers had yet to droop under the weight of progeny. I couldn't help my conqueror's stride—it distanced me from the desert and her. Blue haze broke on the distant rim where a Roman aqueduct anchored a far shore, and the train from France penetrated the Moorish frontier.

The French rail cashier had asked me if my ticket was for the frontier. I'd flown from the American West where my family had lived in a desert tent for over a year, and didn't know Europeans meant *border* instead of a place for my father to escape the Cong, and lose the illusion of share croppers' kids getting a piece of their own. The relics of war blew ashore in tropical depressions—my brothers and I couldn't know our somersaults looked like men catching mortar rounds, as rockets whistled over the wire from bamboo battlements; we were all soldiers in the siege. No one descended to wrestle until dawn by the bank of a dry wash. Redemption in the shade of a rock never lasts.

The desert is wide, exposed, and someone could wander for days fixed on the horizon arriving nowhere, emerging everywhere. In the desert I met her, and we sucked water from cactus pulp and pollinated blossoms under the heat and hate of adolescence. We sketched figures in the sand, searching for why holy men hallow wastes. On the motorcycle, the curve of her back arched breasts high into my shoulders, straining for kisses. It was a trip to die on. Heat exhaustion preyed in the shadows and we painted different visions of the day.

Spanish girls in American jeans danced, stomped and snapped their fingers through summer air. The crowd raised a coliseum cheer—like when the hometown boy sticks a dagger in the foreigner's throat. Colored blouses twirled in light, smiles and winks, señoritas swirled around ringing guitar chords, castanets clacked allegro assai staccato as satin hair blurred, drawing arcs before the bulls. Hoof-struck stone vibrated as horns like soaring scythes slashed through white cotton and blood colored sashes. I wanted a café con leche and a Cruz Campo Beer, wired and altered in a Byronic vision. The smell of blood, vomit, and shit was trapped in the street. I tasted the bulls' dust that hung golden around them. When life hands you death, you have nothing to give back.

And the winner is—the Academy Awards played live on t. v., as we farewell fucked each other like it was the first time under L.A. twilight, because what else were we supposed to do when she moved out to be on her own after three years of thinking we would never tire of the beach, and each believed it was the final one, because it wasn't fucking that faded. We had never married, our own oldest friend, and groped between the madness of possibility and nostalgia—missing each other while sharing air. Haze of chamomile and sandalwood rolled blue in candle light, we *sweated* the smell. Rhine wine stained sheets. Her new boyfriend worked a counter in Westwood thinking I'm riding the high desert horizon beyond El Cajon into the depression of Death Valley. It's never said—everyone knows who the losers for best actor and actress are.

Something romantic in the ear about Spanish frontier, *yeah*. The rail station was loud with violins, guitars, and steel, as backpacks and business suits, legionnaires in stiff kepis blanc, and Euro-hippies dragging ragged cuffs fold francs for their passing of musicians. I spent the night before on a hostel's floor while a Vietnamese kid squatted and beat-off to porn under a Victorian lamp. In the morning, I dropped out a window. Post cards and travel brochures never mention gypsies waving broken bottles, Brazilian prostitutes, live sex shows, or street performers fucked up on hashish, but should.

Sex under the underpass—the last of the farewells—exquisite outside Barstow's exit, as far as she'd go before I had to ride the Vegas bound bus saturated in the dark odor of wine and orgasm. The two of us, swaddled in the red interior of her gray F-150, the windshield confused with steam the defroster couldn't clear; we talked of later, but not like when we rode, kissing through motorcycle helmets at eighty. I hadn't realized love had swallowed so much. My passport, empty.

Muscles under shadowed hides, swollen offerings for the matador, and brown skin wet from bodies are twisted and crushed—sliding on stones splattered for tradition's sake. It was hot, the sun an inquisitor. A woman spun, hands high, reaching her arms toward the sky, then to me, hips flamenco out of reach of bulls and I hesitated at the plaza, caught by the glimpse of black hair like a mirage under the Spanish sun. Bulls and her merged and blurred, voices twined with music—the raw rush of hooves, the rapid tap of high heels in the open air cantina—and I didn't know which was more terrifying or alluring.

Surrounded by frontiers, *chingalos*.

YOU HAVE A BEAUTIFUL
DAUGHTER

Be not afraid of sudden fear.
PROVERBS 3:25

Why? I ask, Why?

The web site for Idaho's Latah County Sheriff says thirty-nine registered sex offenders live in or around my community and four of them live in the Paradise Apartments. You see the mug shots. Fuckwads staring out of the computer screen caught by a camera and as you walk or drive about town you try to recognize them in the maddening crowd or alone walking down the street like some drifter without the high plains. But then at the park with your two daughters--Hey there's that guy with the beard and ponytail, the skinny one, driving a Mustang. Does he drive the fast car because it attracts young girls?

Maybe boys? You can't help but think of those tinted windows rolled up and the damage that car could do in zero to sixty seconds. He still has that grin on his face like in the mug shot: *yeah I'm registered, bitches, but I'm Free.* And lo a short way past the tree, you see the car parking on the street that had been circling the block like the shark around a school of fish. He parks, adjusts his ponytail, just hanging out, watching as your daughter runs, as she imagines the hooves of mustangs over open range. In the warm fall day, ice fills your gut.

When strangers walk up to you and tell you that you have a beautiful daughter, at first you think, *Wow, I have a beautiful daughter.* Then, as she gets older people, usually men, say, oh she's going to be trouble later, I hope you have a shotgun. You discover her beauty attracts praise and predators. Of course after thinking this and nightmares with chocolate, gingerbread men and puppies, you realize nothing will stop a molester threatening the blood of innocents. Everyday beauty and terror, every fucking day. You watch and you look, even at home, at night the odd noise, especially after what happened in Utah and Florida, right out of their own house, gone and sometimes you look too quickly and your daughter's not there; it's like looking at a gun pointed at your head. Then you have a second beautiful daughter.

"Nobody can be awake and asleep at the same time."
                                        Jose Saramago, *Blindness*

My father always said if anyone messes with your family you should kill them or fuck them up so bad no one will mess your family ever again. Like Machiavelli's advice of exercising control through fear where everybody knows who did it, but nobody can say it. Like a hillbilly cosa nostra: blood feuds, an eye for an eye, all *sub rosa* in the piney woods. My grandfather killed a man down in Tennessee back in the twenties over a slain cousin during a bootlegger's argument. Dad said, "Blew a hole like a rosebud into the back of his head." My mother likes to brag that her three sons and husband would avenge her and finds satisfaction of vengeance even if she isn't around to savor it or even if everyone dies—a revenge tragedy. So much the better. I have heard countless parents say, "They mess with my babies and I'll get them. I'd die for my babies."

In the park Sophia faces down two boys her age, challenging them to race, playing to her strength. A crisp breeze rattles the leaves and the sky is washed blue, casting no cloud shadows—a great day for a run. Madison plays in the sand. Sophia sprints and neighs; she believes it gives her power. She reaches the tree, turns and the snot-faced boys are not even a quarter of the way. The man with the ponytail watches. I see him.

Some believe nothing says love like bloodshed.

"Vengeance is mine, sayeth the Lord."

Romans 12:19

"Protect us from sudden death; Give us peaceful lives."

Władysław z Gielniowa

And you never can tell what the bad will look like. Who do you look for? Lucifer was the most beautiful of the

Angels. The Morning Star and fell all of a summer's day, which, to my mind, puts heaven within driving distance to hell. I like to think Lucifer fell through the heated cumulus clouds pushing like explosions up and up, and when he punched through, dragged rain and hail with him and the beautiful lightning.

"But wherefore thou alone? Wherefore with thee / Came not all hell broke loose."

Gabriel to Satan. John Milton, *Paradise Lost.*

"The bitch about it is that rogue waves look like all the other waves until they get up on you. You almost never see them until it's too late."

Skipper Dave Clarke, F/V Seanna

Clouds rake the sky like gray tilled fields. A cold east wind blows and snow spackles Moscow Mountain. The strips of sunlight break through and I see clear into the blue, while dingy stratus clouds obscure the view. I am dizzy and cold and feel the spin of the earth and want to throw up in great oceanic swells. Along the horizon the cumulus clouds are a herd of blue gray sheep grazing the tree line, a blurry border. In one part of the sky, some lenticular clouds are smoothed by high winds, while, in another part, stable air creates sheets of clouds. It is me, and I it, between long cold space and not having the eyesight to see out of town.

"It's always the stuff you don't see that'll get you."

Fire Helicopter Supervisor,
Clearwater National Forest.

"Who would shoot a turtle?" The five-year-old daughter Sophia asks as she squats down to inspect the shell. Of course we know why: people randomly kill things, like those sexy-assed wolves loping in the woods between here and grandma's house that might eat six out of twenty animals they bring down. We are at war and some folks feel they need to practice their amphibian warfare. Probably a kid going into the Marine Corps, dreaming of medals and thinking *I get to go and fight* and it all started with one turtle the size of a Cadillac hub cap—an old school Caddy like we sang about in the army: "Momma, Momma can't you see what this army's done to me. Used to drive a Cadillac, now I pack it on my back." That turtle is collateral damage, baby. Didn't even see the bullet coming. Died for our freedom. We tell the kids that people do bad things for no good reasons, and we don't say, like the way lightning can blow someone's feet off thirty miles away from the storm.

"Did you know *if* is the middle word in life?"
Dennis Hopper as the photojournalist in
Apocalypse Now

Sophia points at the little turtle pressed into the sand like a bottle cap. She asks, "Why did the turtle get run over?" We don't say that the lazy fat ass couldn't stagger four feet from his golf cart, or his drunken wife who'd rather show off her support for that Californian Jeff Gordon in her custom painted cart than walk. The turtle got run over because it got caught on open ground between its mother's egg and the cartless water of the Pamlico Sound. If the turtle was quicker, if the cart was slower, if you hadn't turned your back for a second, your kid's black and white photo wouldn't be hanging in the Walmart entry way. We see those pictures all over, all over and over and think over and over, if you can keep your mind about you when all about you are losing theirs. But enough of Kipling—when Sophia was born—a terrible beauty was born in us, and it was close to Easter and in April that month of "breeding lilacs out of dead ground," and so many uprisings occur in hospitals and Donald Hall called his first born "My Suicide." It was a beautiful suicide; all the nurses said so. Dante was wrong. "Abandon all hope ye who enter here" should be inscribed above the hospital door because, as Jim Morrison said, "No one gets out of here alive."

> Home is the sailor, home from sea,
> And the hunter home from the hill.
> Robert Louis Stevenson, "Requiem"

Poor damned turtle.

Incidental killers are still killers and predators that eat salad are still predators. Paul Shepard said, "Vegetarians are trying to reinvent biology to suit an ideology." Where do they aim their bifocal vision, claws and incisors at night? Are all those feelings of walking the first veldt gone? It takes a predator to get a predator, even though we hunt different things. There is an ontological imperative cobbled into our chain link that keeps our wolves loping around inside the moral wire of our mental zoo, yet still fires us with the desire to run open fields to run something down to hear it scream.

YOU HAVE A BEAUTIFUL DAUGTER

Tyger Tyger burning bright,
In the forests of the night;
What immortal hand or eye,
Dare frame thy fearful symmetry?

William Blake

"I shot a man in Reno just to watch him die."

Johnny Cash,
"Folsom Prison Blues"

We collect seashells and Sophia and Madison want to know where the snails and sea creatures are. We say they moved out to bigger and better houses and Sophia says, "Why would a snail leave if it already had a beautiful shell?" The soft bodied animals, dead, eaten by starfish and crabs and sand fleas, chambers cracked and rolling up on the beach. The girls are like Marianne Moore's paper nautiluses constructing thin glass shells of what we tell them along the shattered glass of the sea. We stand along the sandy strand:

They cannot look out far.
They cannot look in deep.
But when was that ever a bar
To any watch they keep?
    Robert Frost, "Neither Out Far Nor in Deep"

Life is a non sequitur.

Madison yells, "Run Sissy. Run Sissy, run, run as fast as you can!" She begins to jump up and down her copper colored hair coiling and uncoiling. Sophia's tawny hair flies straight, her smile grows as she finishes because the boys still haven't reached the turning point. She laughs and gallops to a tree further off, neighing.

The man with the ponytail lifts a soda and sips from a straw. He smiles, scratches his beard. His door opens. You imagine the click of the release, the creak of the hinges. He steps out, carrying a fast food bag with his soda, and you figure how fast you can run, carrying Madison in your arms to the car before it can drive away leaving only a shroud of smoke. He hips the door closed then starts walking across the grass toward her.

All of our mazy minds spin into a central point where it knows a monster lives, waiting in the dark for the sacrifice from Athens. Blake says, "Cruelty has a human heart."

Irrational forces work in the world requiring virginal sacrifices and those underlying assumptions that create the sex trade and of women chained in basements, of pornography and snuff films and of fathers clutching photos and those sex criminals that come in the shape of friends and relatives, shifting like werewolves beneath a full moon, those fuckers whose flights of angels will not sing them to their rest. One phone call and some losers from Down East will show up and make art of their fucking brains on the carpet—mixed media. You have friends who drive mustangs too and can follow that thread of highway. But your friends are the terrible and the beautiful because they make artworks in the world with an animalistic righteousness that does not question the morality of bashing a molester's brains in with a chain, creating a latticework of bruises the colors of storm clouds, lacy bloodshot flesh, and fine spider web fractures on bone, leaving a modern art drip painting of sweat, blood, semen, urine and shit on a drop cloth not named *Lucifer* by Pollock, but entitled *Retribution* by anon, because even though we do not say it aloud, we love violence to atone for sin, the divine flying in of archangels beautiful and terrible with their goddamned flaming swords—the original Shock and Awe. And behold, Death rode forth with three friends in a white Mustang smeared with smog and grime, dirty with fast food litter the floorboard. Beware modern day the Titus Andronicus using a microwave.

"If you hit a guy with enough voltage he gets a hard-on despite the pain."
CIA operative, Central Highlands, Vietnam 1966.

"God has little patience with remorse."
Malcolm Lowry, *Under the Volcano*

Air, a nothingness, a breath and after the damage is done "what good amid these?" Walt Whitman asks. What good indeed? When, as Dostoevsky points out, hussars would point pistols at infants' mouths and play with them until they smiled, then shoot them in their mothers' arms. "What good O me so sad recurring?"

"I, too, believe in the death penalty. I would like nothing

better than to see you die, Mr. McKinney. However, this is the time to begin the healing process. To show mercy to someone who refused to show any mercy. To use this as the first step in my own closure about losing Matt."

Dennis Shepard

I, too, would like to see myself as merciful because I am not a modern Prometheus. I cannot breathe consciousness into dead flesh or the dead minds of those only aware of their cock and their desire. Compassion has a human heart as much as cruelty and there is no straight biological compulsion for why the same heart is cruel and compassionate—no Cartesian dialectic—No Hegelian antithesis, thesis, synthesis. It is all synthesis waiting outside the light, arms to comfort, arms to crush out breath. It is both terrible and beautiful in the same moment. That point where philosophy fails and all we see is the graceful undulating strides of the lioness in full flight. Who are we fucking kidding?

"Every day I have the blues." B. B. King

"The point is not to mind." T. E. Lawrence

The point is I do have to mind because my girls are un-aware of the lens focused on them. I have to be looking for the lens.

I swing Madison into my arms. She screams, "Let me go," because she wants to play in the sand. I feel a state away, slow and unarmed. The stranger looks as Sophia runs towards him. I will break his arms so badly that he will never hug again. I run with blood pumping in my heart my Madison screaming to let her go. I still run. I will jerk him back by the reins of his hair. I know that son of a bitch is the one in the picture, by that same self-assured smile he grinned at the webcam. I will wreck that mouth. Madison screaming and now crying. "Turn me loose. Turn me loose." She chants like she is calling forth divine providence. Sophia passes by him and reaches the tree her hair streaming behind her, tawny as a deer hide. He heads toward a bench where a family has gathered. The family smiles, wave, greeting the man with the ponytail. They look at me as I still run. I stop and put Madison down as she continues to cry. The family looks uncomfortable as they cast quick glances over hunched shoulders and huddle around the picnic table littered with birthday gifts, hung with balloons, but minding their own business. Maybe they know I am the father or maybe the only thing we fear more than missing children is getting involved. Would hate to spoil the party that I am already dampening. Sophia reaches the tree, pirouettes, her arms thrown skyward, then paws at the air with her hands, shakes her head, neighs and heads back to me as Madison runs for the swings. Everyday beauty and terror, every fucking day. There are 39 registered sex offenders within two square miles from where I stand, and I can't recognize a one of them.

Fever and Guts

II

You swim the sea and you see your daughters on the swells like buoys. They have lights on their heads and they flash, Red and Green. Pass between? Red Right Returning? You need to remember how to get back. Not run onto the shoals, find that channel back. They wave their arms, flash green and red, showing you the channel, but you need to read the signals correctly. How did you get so far out to sea? Did you not account for the tide or the current or both? Did the wind sweep you out? Papa, this way. So many things can cause you to foul your dead reckoning. A wind with brightly colored hair?

You wanted not to dream. Why must sufferers of fevers dream feverish dreams to be awoken by stomach spasms and the bleep bleep bleep of text messages *Sorry you are sick* You wonder about the broad, gray line between love, and not hate, but of the wandering heart, of the distance you worked apart and in less than a month after the break-up says she misses you. You don't want to understand, but you do. You realize you will be friends for years. Love doesn't end with distance just because the body's need to feel another is like gravity. It's as natural as falling. You, strewn in a bed she bought, but never shared because she had it shipped to you in anticipation of her homecoming.

You are laid out on the Antarctic Plateau, gasping for air at almost 10,000 feet above the sea. Steam rises and water puddles around your body and you sink into a melting shaft of ice. Never were you so far from your daughters as when you worked there. Against the thin sky and sundogs that stretch rivers of rainbows thousands of miles, they circle above you, refracted through the minute ice crystals, called diamond dust, frozen out of the air like shore birds, but there is no life at South Pole. Not one creature, insect or bird or mammal except for what people bring there. Bleep, Bleep, Bleep. Your eyes open, the sky is gone, but your eyes still hurt. *I still miss you* Your body stutters as sweat runs from your forehead. Does she mean what she texts or is she just trying to make you feel better?

Perhaps both. The body and the heart can be in two different time zones. The mind twines itself to you and the emotions of the mind and body stretches back like a highway you've been over and it was the most wonderful goddamned stretch of road and you have to keep going, but... *Miss you too. Thanks* You wonder at the degrees of meaning of thanks. Thanks for missing me. Thanks for the bed you now shiver in. Thanks for being sorry, some, all or nothing, a typed word empty and flaccid as a popped balloon. Your daughters know you and their mom are split, but not about the ex-girlfriend and they never will. You dream of her with pink hair streaked with blonde like sunrise flooding over a foreign city.

Conception in a Time of Cold War

"SHOOT TO KILL, KILL FOR THRILL!"
An Army Call and Response.

The drill sergeant stood over me. Under the summer Kentucky sun, I was in the front leaning rest, which is neither leaning nor rest and the world knows as the push-up position or missionary depending on your inclinations. The sergeant yelled, "The best part of you ran down the crack of your mama's ass and left a stain on the backseat of your daddy's car." I was shocked and dumbfounded and not just for being confronted with such a disturbing image of my mother's anatomy nor the insult, as my father had routinely pointed out my flaws in such ways, but I was stunned at his presumption that my parents had done it in the backseat of a car, which of course they had. In my naiveté I didn't realize that in the early sixties the car culture was that pervasive and uniquely American and the drill sergeant probably had an eighty percent chance of being right, no matter which of us sorry jackasses sweating and quivering in the front leaning rest he picked out. Neither of my parents had a car, but horniness makes beggars of us all so a car was borrowed.

My dad owned a car back east. He had recently arrived in Arizona from Kentucky as a door gunner in a helicopter to be stationed at Luke Air Force Base. He was set up on a blind date with my sixteen-year-old mother. He caught rides with pals, hitchhiked, and, of course, borrowed cars. I don't even know what kind of car they ended up in. I imagine it had long swooping lines of two-tone-paint, a chrome grill the size of a bear trap, and tail fins, but it was probably a shitty Rambler with bald tires. Although I was training to fight the same threat my father had, we would find out that this was the height of the Cold War, right after The Bay of Pigs, The Cuban Missile Crisis, the Assassination of J.F.K. and before the Gulf of Tonkin and the large scale deployment of U.S. military forces into South Vietnam, although we did have advisors there and the first American soldier had been killed there in 1945, the year my father was born. This was the era of mutually assured destruction (MAD), a time of annihilation in thirty minutes after the sirens wailed if you couldn't reach a fallout shelter, a time of pent up tensions where young girls swooned in a moment of passion by smooth talking southern boys who vaguely sounded like Elvis. Or at least in my family.

The drill sergeant, apparently not satisfied with the

volume of my "Yes, Drill Sergeant" response to his insult, took the added measure of shifting his boot forward and onto my hand. "I can't hear you," he yelled.

His insult struck me that my finer qualities never even made it into me. I am composed of my father's inability to shoot far and his poor follow through and my mother's reckless inhibition and inability to say no or at least cover that thing. I am the sum of poor planning through passion. My father and mother married in October and I was born in May eight months and three weeks later—very nearly scandalous. Although no one has said so, I figured I was at the wedding. I was not premature, in fact most first pregnancies go long. It's as if the firstborn wants to kick around and stretch out the womb like the early Europeans before the virgin forests of the New World. The first of worn hand-me-downs for the second child worn with a sense of entitlement of someone marked as first.

Perhaps this is why my father favored his next son—both second sons—and they could commiserate the tyranny of the first son in the world, ruining everything he leaves behind with a callous disregard that others may need to follow. But that's what you risk when you unleash an army without thinking—the best is dribbled away and the worst create a scorched earth out of someone's motherland. My mother assured me that I was a difficult pregnancy and she had to make numerous visits to Major Love, the Air Force Doctor.

All of us recruits looked like a field of right triangles kept in shape by our trembling arms. The drill sergeant's boot threatened to collapse the triangle of myself into a parallel line with the ground. I have yelled at the top of my voice and still the drill sergeant yelled, "What's the matter,

Mathes? Haven't your balls dropped?" My name has been interchangeable with epithets like bitch, dick, cunt, pussy, and asshole, making it its own curse and that was before I reached Fort Knox, so the drill sergeants did not bother me. My father often said we'd always be losers because we were Mathes, and nothing ever goes our way. We lose, and no matter how hard we try, we'll never make it. My birth weight was 7-11. You'd have thought that would've accounted for something. I have wondered if the curse only follows from a life of decisions flying on impulse—shooting from the hip or with the hip. There is certain amount of hubris in thinking the only reason you can't succeed is because of some outside force and not a lack of foresight and planning on your part. After all if your very name is a curse borne of slip shod meta-physical forces you can be absolved. All of us bastard children like to think our woes were the woes of our fathers and their fathers passed on curses like a venereal disease. Conception as an STD—a supernaturally transmitted damnation. Why let the lack of one little condom stand in the way when pressure's at the wellhead? Who's got time to run to the store? In thirty minutes everyone could all be dead. Just lie back and enjoy the air rich with honeysuckle.

The drill sergeant, tired of toying with us, took his boot off of my hand and told us to recover, and we all jumped to our feet without doing one push-up. I am the sum of all my flaws, but unlike nuclear war, it is not a zero sum game. At the end of my basic and advanced training, I would be named the honor graduate, the top of my class, cursed name and all that hasty, hair-trigger breeding. My conception, oh child of western deserts, of hot nights, mini skirts and nylons and the backseat-front-leaning-rest, is as American as Imperialism in the guise of defense, the short sighted-American Post WWII Dream, teenaged hubris, life out of the fear of imminent destruction, and ultimately, shooting to thrill—from the hip of course.

MOVING IN GANGLAND

I spent a lot of time drunk, or recovering before payday, and not sleeping. It was Vegas, the Vegas of a disillusioned ex-soldier, college drop-out, who knew Hemingway and Twain eschewed the system—and those guys could write—but in place of fifty-cent imports and no last call, where the city's official color is anything anodized and glittering, where thousand mile wide sunsets were obliterated by mountains of neon illumining false fronts and make believe, defunct civilizations, erasing the night as if when God said *let there be light*, he forgot to say, *and a little night too*—it was easy to derail. My dad's brother, Tony, was only two years older than me, and, in those days, I hung out with him: drag races, casinos, concerts, and stripper bars.

A stripper, Clarisse, asked us to help her move. We knew her from a local club, and she was an exception to small club strippers. She *had* the showgirl look, a high tensile strength body and hair as thick and dark as the insides of bars she danced in. She asked us for help one night, offering us money that we refused. She only had three hours to get her stuff out of the house; she didn't want a confrontation with her ex. I understood. Relationships end in stages similar to death: anger, animosity, sense of failure, reunion delusions, resentment, and, depending on the couple, life-long bitterness or an eventual realization that the other person was never that bad, acceptance.

When my ex-wife and I had become as close as two indifferent people can be, we divorced, and she moved in with her lover, Christine. As most marriages dissolve like a ship ramming a polar ice cap—everyone can see the unavoidable and all aboard can only grit their teeth and pray for minimal blood loss—we melted under the pressure of our passions. We laid ourselves bare, burned all we had like a star collapsing in on its fire and exploding outward into the vacuum, with the roar and thunder blunted by space. We fought against the indifference, the vacuum, thinking that by putting up a fight we could show how much we wanted it to work when we didn't, and somehow assuage the guilt of lovers and suicide attempts of pooled blood and long streaks marking apartment doors like Passover— a surprise for the Holy Ghost to spare the first marriage. We became id. I popped the clutch, burned rubber, motorcycle wheelies between shots of Everclear, and dragged my knee leaving flesh and denim on the road's center strip, and we passed through the ritual of breaking-up by breaking down and lashing out, not knowing how to let go, not wanting to, but wanting to without admitting it aloud. We ground our ship into sawdust and relented because we had nothing left to relent with. We discovered relationships never end, they only change by degrees.

After the hostility was gone, and we could smile at each other again, her mother sued me for pain and suffering I had caused *her*, not to mention she wanted recompense for everything she had bought me during my relationship with her daughter. I threw the papers away and never heard if I lost in court or not.

I was all for no confrontations. My uncle assumed that because we were two guys, who had been in a few fights, that her ex wouldn't want a confrontation either. After all, he may not want her to go, but odds are he wouldn't risk an ass kicking when he could wait until we were long gone. Vegas is all about playing those odds. Being drunk, though, you can never figure all of the possibilities, especially in the erratic nature of broken relationships. I had worked with a guy, Red, at an injection plant. He helped a friend retrieve some possessions from an ex-wife one night after swing-shift. Night is not the time to move. New boyfriends can be armed and jumpy, knowing husbands might be in the anger stage of the break-up. Red took two bullets to the head. His twenty-three year old widow, two-year-old twins in a stroller, wore his motorcycle jacket to the funeral: ashen, blonde, and stoned. Guys became anxious to console her grief.

Sunny, a Vegas hot winter day, and we pulled up in front

of a single story, half-acre house in Tony's factory green, 1964 Dodge Dart. It was a nice neighborhood. Kids played on quarter-acre lawns of imitation ranchettes with split rail fences with wagon-wheel accents. Landscape trucks crowded curbs, and tanned men and women pushed mowers, raked gravel, and clipped hedges.

We each had bottles of Gatorade—trying to soothe dehydration headaches and three hours of sleep—black rock-and-roll tee shirts and jeans, torn and dirty. Clarisse had a small moving truck and was carrying a box with a pale blue boa hanging out of it I had seen her dance with. She walked in heels across the lawn. Her face showed no marks of rouge or lipstick, and she wore an oversized sweater that fell mid-thigh, making her shapeless, although her jeans were tight enough to show she had strong calves. After loading the box, she gave each of us a big hug and told how happy she was that we showed up. She smelled washed, free of perfume, cigarette smoke and the stink of drunks. We helped her with small items: a rocker her mother had given her when her first son was born, pictures of her two kids and family members, hand-carved salt and pepper shakers, a small sculpture of Don Quixote, some books, travel magazines, a record player, and a few Frank Sinatra albums. I was going to ask about her kids, when her husband showed up. She was packing dishes for one.

Tall, Italian, and he wore a suit that needed to be a little bigger in the shoulders. On his left cheek was what looked like cigarette burns. Smooth scar tissue puckered and broke the contour of his profile. The spots were lighter in color than his dark skin and they trembled over a clenched jaw.

He glared at us as he leaned against a bar off the

kitchen, trying to get her to speak to him, he yelled in whispers. His whole body poised as if he was holding back everything he had, but she walked around him, without making eye contact. I heard his teeth grind and, as his physical strength did not work in restraint, he became a well-dressed, brooding bronze. We witnessed the end of how he thought his future would be. Until that moment, he believed in the habit of her reconciliation, but replaced lost faith with nothing, sacraments of dust and water. He hurt, and I felt like a shit head for being there. I couldn't even reach out a hand and commiserate. As fine as the line between empathy and betrayal is, it is even thinner between a gesture of kindness and an insult. Clarisse followed us to the truck and warned us not to stare at the scars on his face; he had been shot and wasn't too happy about it, although he didn't mind the body scars, she said. The atmosphere thickened.

I worried. The sulking guy by the bar could be calling a couple of business acquaintances. While he's vacationing on a Caribbean beach, my uncle and I are vacationing in a shallow grave. Vivid in my mind was Anthony Spillatro. He was involved with a strip club and reputed to have ties to the Mafia, even if it's said there's no Mob in town. One day he came up on a missing person's report and, then, on a day much later, authorities found his body in a Midwestern corn field without his head. There was an ineffable menace, and however tough I thought I was—I knew I wasn't that tough. I had been shot at before, but the odds of bluffing your way past five guys with forty-fives, who fuck people up for a living, are the worst odds in town, a shell game where the ace is a real bullet. I wanted to fold the hand. I wasn't even sleeping with this woman, and here a guy with gunshot wounds on his face looked at me like I'm the son-of-a-bitch. The acid in my stomach burned down into my testicles, and the air became stale and salty in my mouth. I acted calm until the last box was loaded. Tony moved in the same mode: don't look frightened and don't stare at his scars; pretend he's a plant.

Clarisse pulled away first. The yellow moving truck blended into sunlight. As we turned the car around, he walked a measured cadence into the yard, to the grass's edge, his right hand twisting a wedding band, and watched as we drove away. A cape of blue exhaust smoke obscured him, the house, a less than perfect day.

SEX AND THE SINGLE
SWIMMING POOL

I am the teen climbing the short ladder to the board, with
the shorts a little too big, the white drawstring hanging
out, pale skin from reading damn 19ᵗʰ century poetry or
mythology in the shade of date palms and singlewides. My
knees, skinned from basketball, gleam like eyes lit at night,
my hair greening up, and I spring from the board, lift my
body high above the blue as a few friends laugh and slap
water, breaking like mica chips through wetted air, and I
hope no one notices my hard on rising as I soar free above
this desert pool on this first trick dive. My friends and I
want a woman like Isis, who searches the river and caves,
for our lost phallus—wrapped and hidden in muslin. We

are on the edge of a mining town, in the middle of a desert and no women will look for us. Under the Mojave sky, groups of teenagers gather poolside under a burdensome sun in our primitive associations, like Aegean city-states or Egypt. As children, we do not know the names of some things until we are adults and then know them like swimming underwater with our eyes open.

I lean back; arms extend from my sides and suspend my narrow chest to the sun. My body soars over the nuclear desert, my cock a mushroom cloud straining to light sky afire, rises from the thin horizon. I stretched against the pain, wondering why trading hands is a sin or why oral sex is immoral sex—virtuosity of pain. Volleyball players and cheerleaders, in bas-relief on beach towels, tan in the sun of my thoughts. I can't find obscenity in beauty, hard lines, crisp curves balanced between two worlds of knowing. No one designed the high school caste system—the hierarchy of cruelty: slut, jock, geek, virgin, goddess, stoners, shop-guys, mat-fags, bullies, theater-fags, punks, and goat-ropers. Athletes move easy in their muscles like the moon in its curve. And the cast-outs and the unhip grew out of the insecurities that bleach our lives. We are all heroes reflected in blue. I begin to angle my feet toward space.

I look like a strung bow above the water, head down, back arched, my cock an arrow. My Mojave pool writes a wet stanza, sexual strophe, classical and justified, but inside fluid, moving as the wet dream and sex, and new formed women dreaming their own nocturnes huddle in towels. A boy's power take-off, we punks talk of Mustangs—Chargers—Impalas, the American passage into the smell of vinyl and semen. Chlorine fumes induce the Delphic ecstasy and prophecies of who is virginal and who is not by the primordial poem of concrete decks and diving boards, of bikinis and one pieces, where young boys hope to glimpse a nipple washed out by a cannonball or swollen, cold, pushing out a fruit offering to be eaten. We boys search for pubic curls at suit edges and cheerleader tan lines—mocha and milk.

The desert star, her legs wet, refracting sun, iridium glasses reflecting onlookers cupping handfuls of sun tan lotion. Promises unfulfilled, like some father's expectations of his son's virility. I peek toward the girls' door, the narrow fissure, wanting where they came from, as if looking for the *City of God* and Plato's promise of a greater reality, something perfect. I only see girls' shadows cast by fires of my imaginings and rumors from locker rooms—the necropolis of my desire—laboring, aching to kiss the City of God on its very gate. I tilt my head back to see the water's surface, rippling chlorine shadows, like no other color in the desert

My feet point up. My eyes have scanned the sky as my body straightens. Vultures circle almost out of sight on thermal columns, fine figures calling the dead. I write the rough draft of my life, free form free verse, color and light and dark beauty abstracted and transient. I have seen everyone around the pool, think of my friend Bob's pasted cuttings from Playboy in loose-leaf binders, like courtiers

painted on a Grecian kylix. Long to lounge in the shade
of blondes, brunettes and low-riding chicas with alabas-
ter brush strokes of rouge. Light of my Californio swimming pool. A painting that passes and blurs—changes
foreground for background and California, not dreaming,
but Walt Whitman, not San Fran, but Desert Center-Lake
Tamarisk-and Eagle Mountain. Not the supermarket in
Berkley gazing at kumquats and young boys, but the concrete cabana in baggies and the short beard of youth and
unexplored swan dives and gainers. Of asphalt basketball
courts and chain-mail nets rusting for want of water. O me,
O him and I exist on the cusp, worried I'll die before sex.
California, not hotel, but singlewides and campers waiting
for a company house. O where are you Emily in your mod-
est suit under awning shade? I wish we could get together
in the weight of your Nineteenth Century solitude. Why
didn't you and Walt hook up? I want poetry against the bit-
ter nurturing of my upbringing. I fall into deep water from
my arc, touch bottom, the plastic filter cap at the lowest
point without breath, below the last breath.

I come up for air. I adjust my cock along my stomach, act-
ing like I am alone, and they look toward me. I am alone.
What then can I know, treading water looking at the girls
treading the poolside like mining town pin ups? They are
a civilization unto themselves. If they let me touch them,
the mystery would not dissolve. It will deepen and blind
me like a star going super-nova, and, after the first dive, I
will still be swimming with a hard on and find no answers
in experience, only more wonder in some sorry Romantic
notion—the flaw of teen boys.

SEX AND THE SINGLE SWIMMING POOL

Where are you William Blake? Rivers are rarer than rich mining claims, but we could drive my Dodge through dry lakes, past Joshua trees, and we'll fish in slag heap shade by a town turning into a spent uranium dump, as if high school chicks didn't glow enough—high and cool. You won't swim William. I'll point out the fat English teacher who lends me books and who I have a crush on. Her wet extra-large tee-shirt clings to her. She sits by her companion from grad school who is beside the flute player I love, but won't tell. I would dive into any of their arms.

I hear you William—*Goddamn right there*. Meaning the two-fisted body-shots, ones flying out of Midwest tornados, hurricanes squalling onto the Gulf Coast, and desert monsoons drenching teenaged badlands, kicked in the balls and spilled in ink. Visceral ink, felt even by the football hero from three years ago, who can buy beer, and works the crusher on the ten-four rotation, cut-offs and skin the color of dirty sheets. He gets off at the pit mine and hangs out at the pool, always looking like he forgot something, languishing inarticulate, knows meaning is in motion, folding map edges, and driving around that first bend he can't see around and hasn't been, that space is infinitely divisible and the arrow never strikes, never stops— it goes on. We can't escape the black hole and we can't help but look for the light it sucks down, relentless and wordless, a music of female laughter—truth behind the shadows. I swim for the cold concrete side and look up.

My God, the sun is bright.

FEVER AND GUTS

III

You should go to the hospital* You unwind yourself like the spring on pull mower or a power saw. The ones that pop off easy, but take an engineer's hand to get spun back into place. She makes you seriously consider if you might be dying. If this is like one of those news stories: Man Found Dead of Bad Tacos. Or maybe you caught this bug in Louisiana when the friend you stayed with contracted some killer gut pain. Does food poisoning come with fever or is that extra like the guacamole? Pain, like your death, is your own. No one can feel it even as they see the signs on your face like a tarot card, the bead of sweat on the forehead, the crinkle at the corner of the eyes, a twitch of the lip. This is the future. Girls dressed in black, sharing what memories of you? Was he a dream?

You curl into a ball in the bed trying to meditate the pain away that ebbs and flows like glaciers of slow undulating rhythms you don't notice until they're gone, like the text messages setting your phone off, breaking the shell of your isolation. Like your ex-girlfriend: bleep, bleep, bleep, *Why don't you answer?* Memories you share with others, even when you are alone, a dark ball submerged and pushing out in all directions like magma trying rise up against a sealed tunnel. Your relationships to those people changes by degrees like the degrees between awake and asleep in the dreamless sleep you wished would come on you. Just blackness until that spiked ball in your gut quits expanding. Unlike the pain, what visible suffering do we see? Your daughters' lonely eyes, their hopeful smiles, the life-raft hugs, and the knowledge you will come back to them, although in the present you hope to see the dawn. *Have you gone to the hospital yet?*

You dream of great muscular struggles. No matter how hard you push or hit it has no effect on people, snakes, or bears, like turning the wheel on a car without power steering. Everything you do is ineffectual, except that their blows don't hurt. Everything is unfazed. A man smiles back at you and at first all you feel is the rage against him and then rage at your helplessness. All that rage and all the power and you go nowhere. Your muscles seize in the effort, but so do theirs and then someone shoots you. Your body absorbs the bullets and spits them out like drops of leaden sweat and you awake with the molten gut pain. All your muscles feel torn and stretched and burn with a fire of forests turning to ash. You didn't hear the texts coming, a flashing light of messages waiting. *Are you there?* *Wish you'd answer.* *?* *I'm worried.* *Okay, I'll be waiting to hear from you.* It'll take you fifteen minutes before your eyes focus enough to read and respond. *I'm still here...* You wonder if those are empty words. What last words did you speak to your daughters?

Ahead of the Flaming Front

August is the peak-burning month in the Northwest. Even when things start going bad in July, fire folk know August is coming. Stories become cautionary tales to warn of summer's fury and lost lives and what went wrong. August is the month of the Great Blow-Up of 1910, which charred 3 million acres, killing 85 people. Ed Pulaski saved his crew by forcing them into a mineshaft and held them there at gunpoint. During the two days some fire fighters got out of the path of the inferno and other groups of fire fighters huddled under wool blankets in shallow creeks as the fire roared around them. It is also the month of Mann Gulch in 1949 where a fire crossed the creek and

blew up, forcing Wag Dodge and his smokejumpers to re-
treat up canyon. Out of sixteen, thirteen died still running
along the hillside. August is the month everyone buckles
down. The heat and moisture combine in the alchemy of
thunderstorms, which shed lightning over mountains and
basins, and forests and ranges tremble in the acid dry air
and smoke will hang thick in the trees long after fires have
passed through.

On an August morning in 2003, Jenny and I stood on
a rock outcropping a third of the way down slope to where
the dozer had carved a firebreak into the ground. We were
lookouts for our squad of firefighters—Chad, Hannah,
Doug, and Scott—digging a handline—a trail cleared to
mineral earth so fire can't burn across it—into the bottom
of the ravine to tie into a line we had dug the afternoon
before from the eastern side. The crew called Jenny and
I the fire twins, both of us blonde, tall and with a lot of
energy, doing pushups when others sat around. The difference being that she was twenty-three and I was thirty-
nine. I became a teacher to her and passed on my stories
and knowledge of fire. The Milepost 59 Fire was burning
east, up and along the south side of the steep and narrow
canyon of the Clearwater River toward the small town of
Kamiah. The fire had burned over 7000 acres, crews and
aircraft from across the U.S. were flown in and a special
supervisory team from Florida had taken over from the
local state district at Maggie Creek.

White smoke clouded the ponderosa pines in the bottom of the ravine like a heavy fog rising into the morning
air. Two helicopters with buckets slung from their bellies
flew round robins from ponds dug into the farm fields.
Flames, slowed by the night and lower temperatures, crept

up the ravine as helicopters dropped water on spot fires ignited from firebrands—embers and other burning debris like pine cones—blown ahead of the main fire. Up canyon from Jenny and I, forty acres of timber stretched to where the ravine rose up to meet the grass and farmland of the Hamilton Ranch. If the fire escaped us, the ranch house, barn, vehicle sheds, at the head of the ravine would be endangered.

The white smoke told us that it was burning through the damp vegetation and not moving fast. Now if the smoke were black and pushing a column it'd be a different story.

I pulled some dry grass from some cracks in the rocks. I held the grass out and dropped it, and the blades trailed down canyon. The fire was burning into the wind, so it wouldn't advance as fast. As long as we paid attention to the smoke column and the wind, we'd have a good idea of how safe everyone was. I told her how we'd have to keep an eye on the wind as it might switch as the day heated up.

Two days before, we set a backfire in Six Mile Creek that needed to burn through the dried timber, brush, weeds, and grass from our handline and join the wildfire, stopping it. It started in the grass, climbed into parched huckleberry and alder brush, and raced up the trunk of the white fir. In a matter of minutes, firebrands carried over the firebreak we had dug to hold the fire and into the timber. I was the last firefighter up the hill; below me was a squad of five helicopter crewmembers—my helitack squad that specialized in helicopter operations—, four volunteers, and one Idaho Department of Lands forester, who was the incident commander (IC) of what was then a thousand-acre. Several outlying homes, farmhouses and ranches had been evacuated. The crew worked down toward the river as the IC started lighting the grass and brush.

I stood on a small bench, before the hill dropped into timber at a 60 to 70 percent grade to the highway. The volunteers, backs to the fire, scanned the unburned side of the handline. Jenny was the last member of my helitack crew. She looked at me and brought her fists together in front of her, flexed, growled, and yelled, "I got your back."

I flashed a thumb up before keying my radio, calling the helicopter.

The helicopter pivoted above the river, the bucket suspended from its belly like a pendulum, and pointed its nose at me on the steep hillside. "I see you," the pilot said.

As he hovered close, I put down my power saw and stretched my arms toward the fir tree. Jenny's long-limbed stride took her out of sight below the hill's horizon, ponytail trailing below her hardhat. After Jenny disappeared, I watched as One-Echo Hotel nosed into the wind, stabilizing the bucket. Two other helicopters dumped buckets of water into the timber below where the lighting was still going on.

Several hundred gallons of water splashed into the handline, short of the tree. The pilot radioed that he caught a wind shift and would hit it the next time. I picked up my saw, slung it over my shoulder, turned and saw the volunteers pounding at flames with shovels and pulaskis. Firebrands sailed over their heads. They zoned into a shovel space of flames, beating and sweating, hard breaths coughing in smoke and dust, squinting into parched earth. They beat and scrambled at fire growing at their feet, missing the rest of the mountain. Fire was surrounding us. The earthen thud of tools sounded larger than rotors overhead. Flames ripped all the way to the ridge's break, as far as I could see, and raced along the contour, a quarter acre wide.

"You can't catch it," I yelled. "Move down the hand-line."

I radioed Doug as I started through the flames. My voice screeched out, smoke and heat constricting my vocal cords, trees began to torch. The smoke and flames mixed with the greens and browns of earth and foliage creating a burst kaleidoscope. Blue slices of backdrop between the trees were stark, and the dull thump of helicopters beat bass to the flame's tenor and the whoosh of trees consumed in seconds. Sap sizzled and popped. I could feel my skin turning red, the fusion of flame and flesh. Walking turned to running. The volunteers had already started their flight and disappeared over the break.

I had read the books by both Norman Maclean and his son John, read the reports by government investigative teams, complete with interviews and speculation, and I had been around fire and knew no one quits with the fire at their back. People always struggled to outpace flames. Even crews in the midst of conflagrations, about to be burned over, kept running, hoping for the fuel break, the ridge top, rockslide, or a pond, as flames sucked the oxygen out of lungs, replacing it with toxic gasses—scalding alveoli. The dead must have believed they could've beaten the blow-up—even those huddled into fire shelters alone with voices around them calling out the names of those they'd never see again.

My boots slid out from under me as I crested where the hillside dropped off. My forward momentum carried me until, for a second, I hung weightless. The power saw, my line pack and gravity pushed me, and I tried to avoid piling into a tree. Dirt kicked up around me. Wild rose thorns punctured my pants, tore my legs, as loose rocks and gravel clattered ahead of me like a bow wake. The air cooled, flowing from the river, drafted by the fire's heat above us. An ash branch slapped my face, and my eyes watered. My line pack helped drag me to a stop as I dug in my heels and grabbed at branches with my free hand. I stopped in the midst of my crew, dust and smoke swirling. The volunteers kept going until they hit the highway, where, in a pullout along the closed Highway 12, three, twenty person hand-crews staged too late in the eastern shadows.

Jenny leaned into the hill closest to me. Above us, trees with leaves of flames looked like Brancusi's *Bird in Flight*. Polished blades the color of tigers lunged skyward, driving black smoke where the flames couldn't follow. The saw rolled off my shoulder, and she stuck out her hand to help me to my feet. By the end of the day, the fire would grow to 6300 acres.

When the others had climbed back up Jenny and I joined them and we lit the burnout down into the ravine, the five of us took turns lighting and the fire burned away from us. The timber was tall and the brush thick in the dried creek. The wind kept blowing down canyon. We slid one at a time into the rocky creek bottom, scattering rocks and dust, to where we had dug the night before.

The burnout's smoke column still bent away from us, obscuring the sun, carrying bits of grass, leaves and twigs in the updraft. Spot-fires burned down canyon. Grass was up the eastside was sparse. We hung out in the bottom and got the brush burning under the trees. Thunderheads built to the west. Over the fire, cumulous developed, but hadn't grown into thunderstorms. Chad climbed the east-side of the ravine to a point fifty yards up, where a rock-slide blocked the fuel to the top of the ridge, to wait for Doug's radio call to start burning back down. The rest of us watched for spots flying out of the timber.

Before Chad was halfway up, a firebrand flew across the ravine and started burning just below us. Doug and I yelled for Chad to climb faster and start lighting, as we popped fusees. I labored up slope to make the mid-point and burn down to Doug, who burned up toward me. The small ember grew fast like watching a rose bloom in high speed.

Jenny and Hannah scouted the timber upstream. We didn't bother with long strips in the thin, dry grass. We wanted to create a buffer of black between the handline and the increasing spot fire. The wind pushed it and the heat from the fire drew it down canyon. The three of us met at the mid-slope. The fire we had hastily set consumed the spot and kept it from crossing the upstream line. We climbed back down to the creek bottom.

The heat from the west side of the ravine sucked wind down canyon. Jenny pointed at the storm clouds building over the fire, and yelled, "Those aren't sheep clouds." We all laughed, but knew if the storm matured before we were done high winds could blow the fire over us. Fire climbed and cracked and popped in the dried alder brush, syringa, wild roses, and burned up the bark of ponderosa pines as if following a trail of gasoline. Sweat ran down our faces and the trees began waving and creaking in the convection column. I smiled at Jenny, but she looked unsure.

"Do you think we ought to climb up?" She had never held ground against such a big fire. Her eyes watered from the smoke and tears dried before reaching her chin. Thunderstorms loomed.

I saw myself in her seven years before, when I stood in the bottom of a clearcut, as fire galloped over a hundred acres and two guys flanked me, smiling into a night fire, empty drip torches hanging in our hands. I had a twinge in my bowels, yet I trusted those guys wanted to make it home too. "No, things are still carrying down canyon."

Ten feet separated the crowns of torching trees and unburned trees, spotted red by retardant. The heat rose in the creek bottom. This was the hard part, waiting for the fire to back away, standing in the base of all the heat with sweat soaking us, and our fatigued muscles stiffening. The air sucked down canyon cooled our backs as the fire heated our faces.

The fire burned hard in yellow grass and alder brush. Engulfed, Ponderosas torched. Trees exploded skyward like rockets consumed by their own boosters. I thought of the fall campfires I had labored over, spark after spark— flame after flame on insensible wood producing coal smudges and frustration. Below us flames were conjured out of dry air. Smoke crowded the trees and obscured everything down wind.

The wind gusted, the fire burned away from us as the smoke billowed and blended into the cumulus clouds pushing up over the fire. We stood in the canyon's shadow, and below the clouds, sunlight still shone on the eastern ridge. I shivered.

We scaled the steep hillside, onto the ridge road and gathered in a staging area by a tanker truck, various other vehicles, and where two inmate crews, and groups of volunteers had watched us descend the far side and rise out of the smoke and fire on their side with scuffed hardhats, smoke stained faces. The thunderstorms came and everyone crawled into trucks as the wind blasted and the sporadic rain hit the ground. Jenny challenged me to the most push-ups in a minute before we ducked under cover.

The next day, August 23, a light rain covered the fire. At its peak, the fire had 431 people configured in sixteen crews, fourteen engines, several dozers and five helicopters and burned 8139 acres, including someone's house. Two fire fighters had deployed fire shelters. They lived. Accountants figured the cost at 3.2 million dollars for the one fire and if asked, I believe the ranchers, farmers, and the citizens of Kamiah would say it was money worth spending. The fire had started when two teenagers abandoned a truck they had stolen and set it on fire. For what reason, I never found out.

In August of 2006 Jenny and Doug were working on the Krassel heli-rappel crew on the Payette National Forest, while I was on Clearwater National Forest when I heard their helicopter went down, killing all aboard. It wasn't until the next day when I found out they were not among the dead. And I'd be lying if I said that I didn't imagine what it was like in the helicopter as it careened out of control into a road along the East Fork of the South Fork of the Salmon River. In May of 2007 I started work with both of them at Krassel, the oldest rookie on the crew. The stories Jenny now told me about her lost crewmembers made me realize how stories create a remembrance to the dead and all the things they did right, and not the things that went wrong, on the fire line and in friendship. How one crewmember was fanatical about using only wood utensils or the other's stash of hard candy in a flight helmet bag, or maybe another had a never ending stream of movie quotes, and all of the small actions and quirks of speech that develop into the micro-culture of a close fire crew. The stories we repeat are not just so we can learn to read the weather or recognize when a fire is going to blow-up, but so that we are able to weather the storms and keep ahead of the flames that threaten us even in the winter when mist drifts through the trees like last summer's smoke.

THE LONELY BULL

In sixth grade I played football in rural Ash Creek, Arizona. My family had just moved there from a suburb of Phoenix and my only prior experience with football was when my dad would toss one around with my two younger brothers and me, drilling me in the chest with hard passes. He'd also play some two-on-two games with us. As the oldest, I always had to be on the opposite team from my father, and I spent a lot of time getting knocked down by him. Of course both my brothers hated being saddled with me and having to learn how to lose with grace and dignity. They preferred to learn how to do victory dances and be poor winners.

FEVER AND GUTS: A SYMPHONY

The hard tip of the football bruised my body, and the ache in my head from hitting the grass left me feeling that maybe I wasn't cut out for the game. I wasn't even good against kids my own size on the playground, having been blessed with the natural ability to drop an easy pass or trip while running. I was so small that other kids could easily stiff-arm me out of the way. At my old school I hadn't played organized sports of any kind; I had played trumpet in the school band. But my father said that in America, if you wanted it bad enough, all you had to do was work hard, and you could succeed. If I didn't want it bad enough, I'd lose, he said, much like America had lost its will to win against the Viet Cong. It was 1974. I supposed he meant I needed to be more like the guerrilla fighters he'd fought in the war.

We were living in tents on forty acres an hour's drive outside of Ash Creek, where my parents hoped to survive off "the fat of the land." Throughout the summer before I entered sixth grade we attempted to build a house — a "hacienda," my father called it — out of adobe bricks we made by digging a hole, adding water, straw, and dirt, and then stomping the mud with our bare feet until it was the right consistency to shovel into forms my father had built out of two-by-fours. My parents' plan was to create some kind of frontier utopia where we would all be yeoman farmers. "A little hard work," my dad said. Unfortunately there is only so much manpower you can get out of grade-school kids ranging in age from five to eleven, none of us skilled in building anything except out of Lincoln Logs, Lego blocks, and Tinker Toys.

Near the end of the summer my siblings and I had to go to school orientation to learn what we'd need for the upcoming year. (The school was K-through-8.) By then we had dug a two-foot-deep foundation and filled this rect-angular ditch with I don't know how many metric tons of rock hauled in the trunk of my dad's Ford Torino from Turkey Creek, some two miles away. We had also stacked dozens of heavy mud bricks next to the big hole. The day we were to go to orientation my mom and dad had us lather up with soap and then sprayed us down with frig-id water from the three-hundred-gallon trailer-mounted tank. The water made my scalp hurt, and we shivered in the early-morning chill, the cold desert night still hanging close around us like hard luck. Mom outfitted my brothers and me in jeans and western shirts and my sister in a dress sewn by my grandmother. We looked a little like refugees from *The Grapes of Wrath*, but we were clean.

Before we left my father made pancakes over the campfire. His pancakes always had a little wood ash in them — at least, we hoped it was wood ash; my father was a chain smoker and free with where he flicked his cigarettes — but they were yummy slathered in syrup and butter. Football tryouts were the same day as orientation. While we ate, my father turned his head from the skillet, squinted through the cigarette and fire smoke, and told me, "You tell the coach you're a running back." I nodded, not knowing exactly what a running back was.

The coach was a short, muscular man with a small gut and thinning hair who also taught science, math, and his-tory. He had the look of a guy who'd played nose tackle in college and hated the glory-hound running backs. When he asked me what made me a good running back, I thought of my father's brothers, with their cigarette-and-whiskey-stained teeth, sitting around watching games on Sunday with Grandpa when we'd lived in Kentucky, where my father was raised. All former quarterbacks, running backs, and wide receivers, they bragged of their high-school gridiron heroics, of long passes and good hands and fast feet. The drunker they got, the longer the passes became.

They talked about how the grass on the field smelled early in the season, with summer still on it, and later as the north-Kentucky autumn stretched toward winter and they hunted for the championship, rising off the frozen ground to throw or catch one more pass. The field in Ash Creek would never freeze. With its uneven dirt and rocks and clumps of dead grass and mown-over tumbleweeds, it looked like the photographs of No Man's Land I had seen in books about World War I. Throughout our season on the Western Front, we would emerge from practices with bloody rashes, twisted ankles (from stepping in gopher holes), and the occasional snakebite.

As I tried to formulate an answer for the coach, other kids tossed the football and sprinted around the field. Some of the eighth-graders looked as big as my uncles. I couldn't imagine bashing into them. They ran fast on long legs that I knew I couldn't keep up with. Even the smaller kids appeared stronger than I was, probably from wrestling calves and stringing barbed wire. The coach stared at me as I stood on the sidelines wondering what to say. All I could think was how I wanted to play the trumpet.

The trumpet had come into my hands by accident in the fourth grade at my old elementary school. Anyone interested in band was invited to the school one evening, where all the instruments had been laid out in the auditorium for the students to examine. Brass and silver flashed under the lights as kids and parents handled saxophones, flutes, tubas, oboes, clarinets, drums, and trumpets. The velvet-lined case and the sharp smell of valve lubrication filled my head with thoughts of marching bands and mariachis. The trumpet was cool to the touch and as smooth as the skin of my palms.

"Give it a try," my dad said. "Blow a note."

I thought of the bugler blowing reveille and the haunting "Taps" in all those cavalry movies with John Wayne. I held the instrument up. The weight pulled my skinny body forward, so I leaned back a little, put my lips to the mouthpiece, and blew. It made a sound like steam rushing through pipes.

It would take a couple of days for me to learn to purse my lips and make a weak note and weeks to understand how to control my breath, lips, and tongue all at once and manipulate the keys to play tunes like "When the Saints Go Marching In," "The Can-Can," "Stars and Stripes Forever," and "Louie Louie." These songs were not like the music my mother and father listened to: country-and-western songs about truck drivers and cowboys, or the Beatles, or Johnny Rivers, almost all of which was played on guitars. When I stayed up late at Grandma's house, she watched *The Tonight Show* with Johnny Carson, and I heard Doc Severinsen play trumpet with the orchestra. That guy had style. Next to "Taps," the tune I most wanted to learn was the *Tonight Show* theme.

There were five trumpet players in our grade-school band, and I made second chair. I wanted to make first chair and worked hard at it, but I still had fun playing. For concerts we dressed in black slacks, white shirts, and yellow vests with a tiger's head printed on the back. The crowds applauded, and we stood and bowed together. Once I even had a solo. I was jittery beforehand just thinking about it, but I practiced a lot, and when it came time for me to stand, I didn't think of the crowd of parents and other kids, or of my music teacher, who knew how it was supposed to sound. I just closed my eyes and played.

The Ash Creek football field had a barbed-wire fence on one side, with coils of extra wire hanging from posts, reinforcing its resemblance to a World War I battlefield. Lizards and kangaroo rats had tunneled under the gridiron, pushing up mounds of dirt as in a minefield. Some cattle had busted through the fence, and flies buzzed over cow patties. Beyond the wire stretched the desert.

"Well?" The coach had one hand on his hip, and the other held a whistle. The sons of ranchers and fieldworkers threw around footballs, kicking up dust. I sweated under my pads.

There was no school band at Ash Creek. My new trumpet teacher had to drive three hours to give me lessons, and he could only do it one afternoon a week. The timing coincided with one of the five weekly football practices. At the start of tryouts the coach had said, "You miss one practice, you can't play."

I didn't understand how one practice out of five could make a difference. "It's only one day," I said.

"That's the rule."

When I'd played the trumpet in Gilbert, the school's band teacher had offered private lessons after school. I told my parents I wanted to take lessons from her, because I wanted to be first chair and was a little irked that I hadn't worked my way up to it yet. My father had made it clear that unless you could be the best at something, it was pointless to waste your time on it. I loved playing music and didn't want it to be a waste of time. My father told me, "Tell your teacher you need to learn how to play 'The Lonely Bull,' because you're not a real trumpeter until you can play it." I didn't let on that I'd never heard the song. I had been playing the trumpet for a year by then and didn't want to admit that I hadn't the remotest familiarity with this essential piece.

When I made my request, sitting next to the band teacher in the music room, she asked, "Do you like 'The Lonely Bull'?" She warned me that it required fast fingers and precise breath control. She was tall and blond and looked down at me with her almond eyes, waiting for an answer. I shrugged. "Let's start with something easier," she said, "and if you work hard, we'll see how it goes." She pointed at the metal music stand. I opened my spit valve and blew some slobber onto the carpet. I never asked her again.

My father was disappointed when I wasn't able to play "The Lonely Bull" after two semesters' worth of weekly lessons. "What do you expect?" he said. "You didn't practice enough." I never made it past second chair.

The football coach looked me up and down as if I were a steer at auction. "Mathes, how about you run on over there and toss the ball around. Get warmed up."

"My father will want to know what position I am when I get home." I was fairly certain the word *home* didn't have to refer to a house.

The coach sighed and said, "You tell your old man that I'll play you where I want. Now get on over there and warm up."

I put on my helmet, kicked at some cow crap, and

walked into a crowd of players on their way to a losing season. The coach made me a linebacker and a tight end. I practiced this new set of skills, but my underdeveloped body didn't respond. I think I wanted to win as much as anyone, but some kids had a talent that couldn't be explained by "They wanted it more" or "They practiced more." I chased after running backs who faked me out and left me struggling to catch my balance as they sprinted for the end zone. I watched passes sail over my head into the arms of receivers at a dead run. I got bruised and bloodied, had the wind speared out of me, jammed my fingers, and bit my tongue. I was knocked down so many times that I learned the best way to fall to soften the blow. A kid on one team we played weighed thirty pounds more than our heaviest player, and it was my job to stop him. My head rang for a couple of days afterward.

When I'd told my trumpet teacher that I was going to play football instead of taking lessons, I couldn't tell if he was disgusted or relieved. He just gathered his music books, stuffed them into a leather satchel, and left. On long bus rides home from away games, I'd wonder why I had given up the trumpet for this. But deep down I knew why: to please my father and fit in with my uncles, none of whom played an instrument, except one who reportedly could play piano by ear, but he always talked about football like the rest of them. He probably wanted to fit in too. Family tradition is a force as strong as gravity, I thought, sucking our childhood hopes into the black hole of our ancestors' past glory. Riding long distances through the desert slumped in a school-bus seat does make a person contemplative.

I still played the trumpet on my own, after I'd completed my schoolwork and the chores of building the hacienda. I walked far out into the desert to practice because my father didn't want to listen to "that noise," and my mother was often stricken with migraines and lay on a cot with a washcloth over her eyes. I blew that horn to the mesquite and cactus, the range cows and coyotes. But most of my sheet music was from band, and the individual parts from a concert score sounded incomplete without the rest.

Playing felt more and more pointless and irrelevant, all alone in the desert, learning nothing new and not sure if what I was doing was right. I ached to be back in the band, to be a part of that bigger group, to be around others who spoke my language and understood me. But, as my dad often pointed out, "You got to make do with what you got." I stood among the yucca plants, under a sky more immense than any I have known since, and played as loud as my young lungs could, the notes swallowed by the big blue expanse. I imagined that some cowboy, catching sight of the sun striking the brass, might fancy he'd glimpsed a city of gold just beyond his reach and heard its herald blow.

My trumpet eventually became the property of a pawnshop. One day I went looking for it and couldn't find it, and when I asked my mom, she said, "Bills needed to be paid. Besides, you weren't using it." I felt cheated because I had still been playing; they just hadn't noticed. But now I think of all the money they spent on lessons and how my desire to play paled next to the need to feed their children.

We had to abandon the land — or, rather, the bank seized it — and take to the road like our Okie ancestors. My father loaded us into a sixteen-year-old white Dodge

Dart with a red hood (the Torino had gone to pay bills too), and we drove off, leaving behind what looked like the ruins of a mining camp: stacked bricks, a worthless hole in the ground, wind-battered tents sagging on aluminum poles. At the time I couldn't imagine the defeat my parents must have felt, being expelled from their frontier Eden. Now, of course, I've had enough bastards beat me down to sympathize. They had wanted to provide for us an example — albeit a nineteenth-century one — of what the world should be like, but the world wouldn't let them, because they didn't have the money.

I don't have many fond memories of Ash Creek, but I'll never forget the afternoons my brothers and I accompanied our father into the desert to shoot jack rabbits and cottontails. He would take his twelve-gauge shotgun, and we would follow him along a cattle trail. Before long before he'd flush one out and blast it. We all learned to gut and skin the rabbits, some of which my father fed to his coal-black Belgian shepherd, or my sister's Chihuahua, or the four kittens he had brought home one day. Others my mom rolled in flour and fried up in a skillet on our camp stove. As the setting sun painted the sky with colors like smeared flowers, we'd hunker around the campfire and eat the gamey meat, tossing the bones into the flames like nomadic hunters.

One day our father shot a pregnant jack rabbit. I slit her hide, and the three kits spilled out, struggling against the membrane of the placenta. I freed them, cradled the bloody, suckling bunnies in my shirt, and brought them back to the camp, where I put them in a box with some scraps of cloth my mom was saving to make a quilt. My mother mixed some powdered milk, and I nursed them with a dropper from an eye-medicine bottle. I was going to raise these rabbits. It is a peculiar thing to do: kill a creature and then try like hell to keep its babies alive. I didn't ponder it too much. For me it was just part of our complex and contradictory human nature.

The first rabbit died that morning, the second a day later. On the third afternoon the last bunny died. I mixed a glass of powdered milk and drank it, then carried the corpse out to where the others were buried and put it in the ground and played my trumpet for all three of them. I was barefoot, feet toughened from mixing mud and straw, and I held the trumpet with hands rough from men's work. I faced my thin, shirtless, desert-tanned body to the west and worked up enough spit to play "Taps," the only piece of music I had ever successfully set out to learn on my own. I flubbed a couple of notes, and I'm certain it sounded horrible. That was the last time I ever played my trumpet: "Taps" for a dead rabbit. I didn't plan it that way.

A Following Sea

Open water in the Gulf of Alaska welled up to forty-foot swells in front of gale-force winds—a storm-warning. Rain drove sideways. Night. The white fishing boat wallowed up a long, watery grade and hove into the wind as the German deckhand, Julia, hooked the buoy, ran the line through the davit, and dogged it off, after taking a wrap around the deck-winch drum amidships. Chuck from Chicago stowed the buoy and hook. Crab-lights mounted on the masthead, switched on, engulfing the *Seanna* in a sphere of light. We couldn't see twenty yards beyond the boat. Wind-ragged flags of shadows blurred from the light's intensity. On a calm day, I could dangle my hand in the water, but during the storm, the gunwale was a break-water. The ocean's wind rippled and pelted surface glowed with plankton. Thousands of squid wiggled tentacles as delicate as infant fingers. They darted between the surface and sight, flechettes bathed in light arising as opaque shadows as if we had sailed into a curtain of sea grass or the bottom had risen to ship-foundering waters.

This was the last halibut derby to be run in Alaska. The tradition of the crews fishing forty-eight straight hours, no matter the weather, was passing. Instead, a quota system would be put into place where, based on past catches, skippers would be given a permit to catch so many tons of fish in a year. Skippers could buy other permits and catch more fish, but there was no time limit. This slower pace meant less crew was needed and many fishermen and women who had fished the derbies in the past would never fish for halibut, lingcod, or black cod again. Dave talked of selling his permit, gear, and tackle. "All the big ships get the majority of the quota, and us little guys don't get enough to make a living, much less cover the cost of going out," he'd said as we readied to cast off ahead of the gathering storm clouds. He worried because he didn't know what else he could make a living doing as fishing was all he'd done since returning from Vietnam, taking over his father's boat. Onboard the *Seanna* we all hoped this last hurrah brought us enough money to see us through winter until the next season. I needed money to send south to keep the electricity on.

What I didn't know, like the fisherman who chafed against changing traditions they should have seen coming, was that my soon-to-be-ex-wife had taken most of the thousands of dollars I had sent south and helped to pay the wages of dealers, pit bosses, floor people, security guards, cashiers, bartenders, cocktail waitresses, and insured the lights kept burning back the thick Nevada night.

I should have known, at least suspected with all the calls for cash advances on uncaught fish. Should've remembered the year before we had fled Las Vegas and creditors, broken family deals and a buffet of addictions for Boise and the Northwest like Lot and Ildeth looking for salvation over the mountains. Maybe more like the citizens of a boomtown gone bust-town, picking up everything and rolling out undercover of night to recreate our lives in a new territory. Unlike Lot's wife, my soon-to-be-ex-wife didn't just turn to look over her shoulder, but marched back into the valley. The anxiety of the future outweighed the risk returning to a failed past. I fished in denial, wanting to believe I had found some utopian love, wanting to trust that I had a future with this woman I didn't want to lose or so I believed. I fished in fear of confrontation and kept my head down, thinking the future that had already capsized would right itself.

Dave emerged from the wheelhouse, revved the engine from the control-head attached on the starboard side-rail, and engaged the hydraulics. His beard streaked with water and age. It was the first night of the two-day halibut fishery. We had set and retrieved gear in the storm all day. It had taken a week for three of us to cut bait, hook it, and coil the lines into foot deep black tubs. My hands ached from being wrapped around a knife for so long.

Portside, I squatted on an overturned tub, facing

forward, sandwiched between the side rail and the hatch
raised waist high above the deck. I had a foot of leeway
on each side and as the boat yawed, I slid, bruising my
upper arms. The wind funneled down the side-deck and
filled my slicker hood with rain. From the deck winch, the
long-line fed through a pulley and into the tub. Julia and
Chuck had knives on the hatch cover. Dave had his gaff
hook. Fishing had been hard and miserable. Sand fleas and
mud sharks had devoured halibut, lingcod, and black cod.
We carried more weight in ice than fish, and the sea hammered us as we ran to find better grounds or recover gear.
We always felt the next set would be the money haul. The
one that'd turn our luck around.

People have clung to the past as a template for a future
even as it slipped away like coins into a slot machine. Who
mourned the Nantucket whalers, the riggers of sails, the
stokers of boilers, the iron-backed rowers, the strong-
armed harpooners, those suddenly without a future, walking the docks, shipless, and no money to send home? It is
more of course. People had tied up their identities in professions and the history of professions and the traditions
of professions. What was it to lose icon status, something
emblematic of an entire way of life, an era, a culture, to
become the dishwasher, the day laborer, the digger of
ditches? To be referred to in the past tense. I was a.... To
lose the present tense, to be. I am___blank—a what? A....
What made them tremble was not only losing the job, but
the fear of losing the self and not finding anything but the
void, to become obsolete and desperate to survive. What
was it like to tie off the last three-masted whaling barque,

the *Charles W. Morgan,* to the dock and walk away?

Dave pulled the winch lever and the motor noise deepened as the knocking diesel slowed. The lead-cored line fed as I looped it into the tub. Hand over hand. I coiled the long-line into the black tubs as hooks the size of shot glasses cut gale force circles around my head. Each hook was only a fathom apart, swinging from the long-line by a thirty-six inch bootlace like leader. Hook, loop, hook, cold water ran down my face and drained out of my beard, soaking my chest; a shark—a two-footer. The mud sharks weren't much—two to four feet long, but they had teeth, a barb at the base of the adipose fin like a dull number two pencil, and rough hide. "Jerry, you'd better not be cutting *my* leaders." I had a knife in a slot on the hatch cover in case of an emergency. My job, though, was to *unhook* the sharks, not cut them free like so many galley slaves after the fall of the Roman Empire.

The crew appeared as shades on the other side of the hatch—hoods up, heads down—struggling to stay afoot, leaning and rocking into the side-rail and hatch. It'd be like crossing the Bering Straits to get to them if something went wrong. A ship of strangers, we fished and lived as close as an estranged family. Dave gaffed a halibut the size of a truck hood and lugged it onto the deck. Julia and Chuck dead lifted the fish onto the hatch, and she started cleaning it. Chuck had the flu and leaned against the hatch a few seconds before picking up a small cod. Big fish were worth more because buyers paid by the pound and one halibut took the hold space of dozens of cod. No one wanted to gut a thousand cod.

Less work and more money. Is the gamble better when it involves hard work? What is the nature of our desire to risk everything, life, limb, or marriage? Sometimes I feel my memory is as uncertain as the future and not because memory is faulty, which it is, but because of our propensity of see it as better or worse or forgetting the crucial detail or conceive ourselves as somehow holding the answers for a future we cannot comprehend. This was why Dave became off kilter when he returned to fishing grounds that had provided large hauls, but found them barren. "Where have they all gone? Everyone who fished here last year had good catches." He wasn't alone. Surprise even when the signs were poking at the edge of consciousness. As our ship drew blanks and steaming from set to set, my soon-to-be-ex-wife was shifting from poker machine to poker machine, casino to casino, desperate and hungry to hear the clanging of bells and coins, the electronic melody of the winner and see the lights flashing for the big jackpot, she knew was possible to assure her future. I pushed failure out of my mind. I needed to believe in the better future, even though generations of people have proven that it doesn't always get better. Indeed, it can get worse in a bad, fast way that leaves a person wishing for divine intervention.

The hydraulics sounded throaty, like a truck downshifting on a steep hill. Swells rose and it was as if we sailed across the great backs of black whales, sounding and diving, blowing spume across the deck. Some smaller fish came over the side, cod, nothing, nothing, nothing, a halibut head, nothing, a shark, a ling head, a small halibut, nothing, several halibut, black cod, sharks—a three footer, a two footer, they're strong. I slid on the deck, my arms beaten and sore, hands cramped as I struggled to unhook a shark, another flipped over, the line balled up, and tangled, my neck ached as if a Zippo had flicked open in my muscle. I cut the shark free. It flipped overboard, swam away—tough fuckers. Gulls shrieked and dove in and out of the light, some floated on the swells and swam for halibut guts and cod heads flung overboard, while others caught jet stream air winging hard like fallen stars—glaring white.

When I left for Alaska, we had high hopes. We bought a ferry ticket, and I was going to ride to Bellingham with the friend who had told me about all the cash a person could make as a deckhand in a short time. "Thirty-grand, man, in just a couple of months," he said. I'd earn a payday big enough in a short time that would enable us to cast off debt and keep us in the lie of trust and happiness for a while. Our bank account held enough money for another month's rent and food. I showed up on a dock in Ketchikan with forty bucks, a backpack and three weeks of dried food assembled from a grocery store's bulk bins. I had thrown my hat over the fence, as the old saying went like some drifter headed West because he heard others were picking nuggets out of streams a fellow could retire on.

My father quit or got laid off from jobs as varied as truck driver to judge so that I never felt part of a tradition, and I drifted looking for anything to anchor me and secure a future. I don't shed tears or wring my hands at the passing of eras, but marvel at new things wrought in the world that never existed before. Some things need to pass and as much as I felt sorry for those who do had to move on, they had to move on. The great square-rigged whalers vanished from the horizons as nothing endures, no matter how many centuries sails plied the seas. In America, the tradition of lighting out for the territories to make a new life was as real as the tradition of generations of bankers, lawyers, and doctors in East Coast aristocracy. As a people we moved across the landscape with the faith that we could make it better from the Asiatic migrations over the Bering land bridge to the great migrations of African Americans to the industrial cities of the north and west. These were all gold rushes of sorts.

With the same faith I knew I could make it in Alaska with a good run of fish, my soon-to-be-ex-wife haunted casinos, believing we were one good run of cards away from prosperity. I couldn't have known that then, or could I? I knew in my guts, saw the signs, like the first smoking stacks of steamers along a Nineteenth Century quay, but ignored them because it was easier to pretend that when I got home we were set. Instead a new storm broke out and with it the last of the excuses. Bills piled on a counter, full of past due penalties for my denial, and bills I didn't even know existed, until the phone calls and letters of collectors my first week home. Even when I quit answering the phone, the last of my willful ignorance eroded away. It was hard to stay in denial when the bank took my car because she had taken out a loan against it to cover a gambling debt. I could have opened my mouth much earlier, turned to face the end I knew was looming, but didn't because it was much easier to be pushed along by a following sea than run against the current and act surprised when I crashed.

Rain ran down my spine after pooling in the back of my hood. Water and sweat saturated my ball cap. I shivered and my thighs trembled like rolled, rusted cable being unwound. Several more sharks twisted into the line. I kept trying to watch how many fish were coming over the side and all the desperation to make the future had no power to make them bite or stay on the hook. My joints became unmeshed gears, grinding cartilage into grit. The bend of two lines came through the pulley. I untied the two sections and started coiling a new tub.

A hook slashed my hood as I tried to switch the snarl with an empty tub. I slipped escaping the hook. My elbow bored into the hatch cover, my fingertips numbed and throbbed. The line overflowed the pulley as the boat rocked. We were a ball of light adrift. We grunted and heaved. We slid and braced ourselves against the jolts of the bucking sea cocooned in rain gear and wind. I blinked into the driving rain and everything was black, except for the ocean's surface glowing and writhing. Salt spray shriveled my lips and gums, stung my eyes. Blood slicked the deck and hatch covers. Hunched over the tub, I coiled, crashed into the side-rail and hatch, looped line, dodged hooks, and grappled sharks like a cast down Greek hero—over and over and over—and whichever way we sailed was dark.

STRIKING
INTO NOTHINGNESS

Ghosts and lightning are essentially air. Ghosts, for believers, are manifest in electromagnetic energy, ectoplasm, which is a bio-plasma and sensed as cold spots or hazy visions in the atmosphere. Lightning is super-heated atmosphere; plasma charged with electricity, although at the same time it is air the way ice is water. And it can split trees and crack rocks and melt sand into glass and strike dead any living thing—antelope, elk, deer, moose, cows, horses, and humans—unlucky enough to be in the conductive path. Mythically, ghosts and lightning are associated with the world of gods, the sky, the metaphysical, and are intertwined with mystery, instilling terror and fear wherever their presence is possible. They both seem to come out of nowhere.

I wish I could see a ghost. I want to believe in the paranormal wanderings of spirits, the immortal residue of the human self, because I am a skeptic and distrust religions and pop culture spiritualism and don't believe the pseudo-scientists or the mystics who spin over detailed cause and effect relationships. I am more likely to believe average people who, wandering around, feel a presence or see an apparition and are struck with belief, like traveling the road to Damascus or sitting under the Bohdi Tree, the final letting-go. Letting go is hard, and the harder you look, the further away the experience gets. The believers' conviction, sincere as it might be, is experientially solipsistic, and I cannot share it. I continue to look, and believe seeing a ghost, if they exist, is like anticipating where lightning will strike. You have to look skyward, where you think it might hit, in both its beauty and its terror as it fractures the atmosphere.

As a wildland firefighter I have seen lightning storms crowd thick clouds with Rembrandt light, backlighting mountains at night, creating thermal images of ridges and draws, and the dark forest looking like hair standing against the whitened sky. On the mountain, the wind blows the smells of smoke, rain, and ozone—the gathering of lightning. On a fire lookout, guy wires, antennas, and parts of the metal superstructure glow blue and shimmer until it seems the room of the lookout floats above the mountains amid the thunder's tympani in a static-charged halo. Lightning-struck trees will flare and torch for a brief moment in the darkness before being drowned in the rain, if there is rain. In the woods lightning has a greater probability of killing a firefighter than smoke or heat. I have heard the snap of trees and seen huge slabs of wood shorn off tree trunks and flung like smoldering spears into the ground as the concussion caused my body to flinch, dropping me to the earth. The force of lightning reminds me of poltergeists. Believers say poltergeists can do things such as knock knick-knacks or books off shelves, turn on and off lights, or shut the door and windows, even scratch and hit people, by manipulating air, making it a force.

The *Six Minutes for Safety* bulletin on thunderstorms produced by the National Interagency Fire Center (NIFC) states, "If you feel the hair on your arms or head 'stand up,' there is a high probability of a strike in the vicinity." This static charge is the air ionizing. Anybody can create this phenomenon in miniature by rubbing a balloon on his or her hair. It is static cling. A common experience is walking across the carpet then grounding out on a doorknob or another person, receiving a low voltage lighting strike. People who have encountered ghosts say before seeing the apparition, they feel their hair rising—a precursor to the shock.

This kind of forewarning reminded me of when I instructed Hwa Rang Do, a Korean martial art, in Downey, California during the late 80s. I taught students, not only the physical world of the art, but also how to control their minds to control their bodies—the invisible part of the art. The martial arts students sat cross-legged in front of me in ranks and files on the blue matted floor, and I told the students to breathe in through their noses in a slow measured cadence, hold it deep in their abdomen below their navels, (dan jun in Korean), and then to let the breath trail out. Each deep controlled breath steered a person to improvement. The students were to think of nothing but the breath, to breathe and count to slow their hearts and bodies, making their minds as still and dark as arctic ice. The air had power.

My grandmaster taught me that controlled breathing was the first step to improving technique, by visualizing each form, joint manipulation, and throw toward unobtainable perfection. Breath control was a means of removing conscious thought from reaction, whereby a martial artist reacts instead of registering events and then reacting, and he taught it was the method for gaining supraawareness. The grandmaster claimed he could feel the spiritual energy of a place, and no one could surprise him. And I believed him. He was in his sixties and could jump, spin five hundred and forty degrees, as he kicked a target six feet off of the ground, and he flipped me and threw me as casually as flicking a cigarette ash. He was famous for puncturing the flesh of his arm or neck with a sharpened spoke and pulling cars, or holding bricks on his head while another master broke them with a sledgehammer. The most important aspect though was feeling the strike of an enemy before it happened. He said, "It is all in your proper breathing."

NIFC also says that you should not lie down, but rather sit up on your pack in the middle of an open field, staying clear of clumps of trees, and "avoid grouping together. Keep a minimum of 15 feet between people when possible." All of which seems counter-intuitive. Imagine sitting in an open field, the wind cold, but building, gusting with the lightning flying and the thunder cracking your eyes shut from the pressure of the atmosphere you can feel in your inner ear; the thunderhead blowing great downdrafts hurling sand, seeds, and leaves; you, exposed in the open when every muscle wants to dash for shelter or huddle with other crewmembers. You can't even hunker down in a ravine or dried creek bed because a flash flood will wash you away. You can't lie down as it maximizes your contact with the ground and if lightning were to strike close, it would travel along the earth and fry you. You crouch alone next to the earth, thighs cramping, and if you are lucky, the bone-breaking hail will not come, only the thick thunderstorm rain, but the lightning will always be there, prodding the ground, brilliant strikes you can see through eyes squeezed so tight the flares are red, busting the air like a sledge on rock, and you as isolated as a ghost on some moor.

In the Hwa Rang Do studio, we would squat for long periods of time to train our legs for endurance and then jump in a plyometric exercise to build explosive kicks. We hovered above the ground, and some students fell over or put their hands down to steady themselves. I never thought training in self-defense to develop the power to lash out would give me the power not to move while the weather lashed around me. But it makes perfect sense. Sometimes preparing the body and mind for the unexpected, leads to unexpected results.

A lightning bolt can strike twenty-five miles away from a storm and kill a person. The National Oceanographic and

Atmospheric Association (NOAA) states, "The '30/30' rule for lightning safety could save your life. The first '30' means that you need to take cover if you hear thunder within 30 seconds of the lightning flash ('flash to bang' ratio). Then wait at least 30 minutes after the last lightning flash or thunder in order to resume normal activity - the 'all clear' signal."

In 1931 this wasn't common knowledge. In north central Idaho, on the backcountry fire lookout tower Bertha Hill (which is actually a butte 5520 feet above sea level), the smoke-chaser Glen Frazier was sitting on a steel bunk when a bolt hit and killed him. His partner Carl Altmiller had been standing on the observation deck after the storm and was struck unconscious. I imagine Altmiller walking out, seeing the clear sky, water dogs rising out of draws and some smokes that he had called in to fire crews or maybe getting ready to go to with Frazier. He might have heard the creeks flooded with rain, smelled the pines and firs as he surveyed the wide, deep draws of the Clearwater Range around the North Fork and the rippled shades of greens and browns of a summer forest. The air might've been cool. Maybe some deer or elk grazed out to the fringe of timber and certainly the birds: robins, jays, the swallows, and magpies would have been active after the storm. I wonder if they felt the strike coming. A former fire warden and several crewmembers of the Clearwater-Potlatch Timber Protective Agency claim to have seen Frazier's ghost over the years and one man, known as Ricochet, will not stay in the lookout after sundown after his experience.

Ricochet, in addition to working as a fire warden, had also worked as a sheriff who got his nickname because if someone startled him, he'd jump. When facing a fire or a criminal he was steadfast. I never worked with him, but he had the reputation that in an emergency he directed resources, prioritized incidents and never lost a lot of acres to fires on his district. Firefighting and law enforcement are reactionary occupations, you have to be able to wait for an unknown event and react, such as I had been taught in the martial arts. These are physical things, while ghosts are not. For him, I imagine, reacting to an apparition was too much, something he couldn't control or direct. Maybe his fear rose out of the elemental place in humans that has driven centuries of superstitions like vampires or ghouls who feed off the living and are almost impossible to stop. I do not know how I would react. I want to think I would watch, glimpse the afterlife, or at least confirm it. For me, the greatest fear is not that a ghost may capture me, but the possibility that I cannot be caught at all.

Ricochet saw another ghost on Bertha Hill. A student from the University of Idaho, Mada Talbot, died in 1966 when she fell fifty-six feet from the lookout's observation deck. She worked the summers for money and lived in solitude, with exception of her large dog. Every morning, leaning against the rail, brushing out her long blonde tangles, she waited for the morning patrol to fly over to wave at the pilot. One morning, as near as any one can tell, her dog jumped up on her, spinning her backwards into the air.

Ricochet said, "I saw her standing there, and I was struck dumb. I waited and squinted and couldn't believe I was seeing a second spirit out there. Her hair swayed and she looked to step toward me, and I turned and ran down the steps and jumped in my truck and drove away."

I have seen neither of these ghosts, and I have been

on Bertha Hill several times, but only climbed the tower once. During June of 2001, I was the assistant fire warden at Elk River, Idaho and was teaching and taking refresher training at a Fire School at the C-PTPA fire camp outside of Headquarters, Idaho. I drove to the lookout with Kurt, the assistant fire warden from Orofino, Idaho. The old gravel road wound through the mountains and sharp draws, through meadows, by creeks and climbed past clear cuts, mature tracts of timber, and areas of replanted trees of various ages. The subject of the ghosts came up during the hour before we pulled up to the tower.

I asked Kurt, "Have you ever seen the ghosts?"

"No." He stroked his thin, red-blond mustache. "You?"

"No, I haven't seen any ghosts at all."

He nodded as he directed the truck over the bumpy road. "Me neither. A few people say they've seen the ghosts at Bertha. Maybe we'll see them today."

"Maybe, no big deal. But, it'd be a great place to be a ghost."

Neither of us admitted that we wanted to see them, but I bet he did just like me, he more to pass into local folklore. Stories about his family in the Clearwater stretched back to the early twentieth century. His father worked for the Association and his grandfather built the first lookout on Elk Butte, by Elk River. A ghost experience would set him apart from his family. As we pulled up top of Bertha Hill, the sky shivered blue and only a few fair weather cumulous clouds skirted the horizon. Kurt climbed the steps forty feet to the landing and unlocked the trapdoor in the floor of the deck that ringed the lookout's room. Steel mesh extended from the framework in case someone else might fall.

I started my ascent, looking through the air for an apparition with each step. My pulse increased as I sucked breath into my nostrils and tasted the air as it released from my mouth. The high country was cool. I strained for changes: visual, tactile, and aural. Rising onto the platform and walking around the deck, I squinted against the sun. I wanted to see her leaning against the rail combing her blonde hair. I wanted awareness sharpened to whatever might confirm some hope in the afterlife. I could see the hazy ridges like a series of waves receding in all directions from Bertha Hill, the patchwork of forest, and all of the hues, grays, greens and browns, of the rugged land. Some mountains toward Montana in the northeast still had snow filled draws and the peaks glowed with ice. A breeze chilled me, but I knew it was only the wind.

We stayed thirty minutes. Inside the room I squinted my eyes, looking for changes in the room, maybe Frazier's form on the bed. I listened, and breathed at a meditative pace to settle my body and mind. I tried not to look like I was doing these things. Kurt opened a cabinet and took out a pair of binoculars. He scanned the horizon through the windows.

The room never changed: the empty bunk, propane lamps, stove, maps, paperbacks, and the alidade for locating fires. It was like when I looked for a field manual on a shelf, but wasn't there. I looked where it was supposed to be, then at the manuals around the space. I even pulled some of the other handbooks and binders off the shelf to see if it got pushed behind, then after putting the manuals back, ran my fingers along the spines, looking again as if it had been there all along and I had simply overlooked

it. In the lookout, only the sunshine of a setting sun filled
the empty spaces.

Kurt put the binoculars away and said to me, "No
smokes out there, yet." Next month smokes would pop up
all over the district from lightning storms building in the
friction of heat and moisture.

We got in the truck and drove away. My hair never
rose nor did I feel the static in the air, smell the ozone,
sense the temperature fluctuate or go colder. I left because
we had to get back to the fire camp. I was out of time,
which is a different kind of fear than seeing a ghost on a
fire lookout, a fear of mortality. I risked my life fighting
fire and being out in storms, and I thought it preferable
to chance sudden death than to risk the slow wait as I an-
ticipated my last breath. After my first daughter was born,
I wanted the lightning strike of a ghost so that I could
believe if something did happen to me, there was something greater than me, greater than the sum of my DNA,
which existed and our bond was more than a biological/
social construct. I also felt the desire to know that she carried an essence, a spirit, which made her immortal, something science cannot answer anymore than religion with
the certainty I need. The plasma of truth condensed into
an awestruck moment. My road did not go to Damascus.
As we drove back to camp, and the mountains and woods
deepened in shadows, I thought of my only experience
with what could be taken as a ghost.

At the Hwa Rang Do studio I met many people who came

from other studios or who came back after an absence. Some of them wanted only to get back into shape, whereas others wanted to be able to defend themselves against the fear of violence. Some came for the mystical and esoteric side of Eastern martial arts, and a few of my fellow practitioners believed a person could sense spirits.

I don't remember where Paul came from, but he claimed he could see ghosts and the rest us of could tap into the vision, if we meditated in a series and followed his directions. A series is where several people sit in a rank facing the wall mirror in the studio and meditate until breathing is in synch, while squinting the eyes until their form becomes hazy in the low light of the studio. This state of mind was supposed to make all of us aware of the spirits in the studio. It was rumored that the spirit of Hwa Rang Do's founder inhabited the studio of the current grandmaster, as did the legendary martial artist/mercenary Michael Echanis who was killed in Nicaragua in the 70s. In essence it was a séance with an Eastern flavor.

Paul, my girlfriend Janet, two other instructors—Carlos and Daniel—and I decided to meet in the studio one night at midnight. Janet and I talked on our way over how hokey the whole thing seemed. I believed in meditation and visualization to improve skills and increase awareness, but I didn't believe in ghosts, and I was an agnostic, although I tried to hold on to the idea of a spiritual world to counter my own fear of dissolution of self. Janet shared my views, but she wanted to humor Paul because he was so earnest. His blonde-brown hair, sticking out in different directions, framed his face, which always looked surprised or as if he had just learned a secret. Paul said things like, "I can see your aura. It's blue." And expected that his saying this was proof he could see some counter-world and had special perception.

We all sat on the floor, several feet apart, as if taking measures against lightning strike. Paul turned out the lights. Ambient light from the street allowed us to see ourselves in the mirror. Late, only a few cars drove along Firestone Boulevard. I squinted my eyes and started to control my breathing. I imagined a stream of gold light entering my nose and circulating in my *dan jun*. I felt it swell before releasing the air, visualizing it in stream of smoke from between my pursed lips.

Paul said, "In breath." Then, "Hold." After a five count he said, "Out breath." He repeated the cycle, and we all started to synchronize our breathing in the warm studio.

I didn't know what to expect. I had meditated a lot over the course of my martial arts career, but this was different. Instead of only turning inward, my concentration projected outward. If successful, I would prove something existed alongside the temporal and corporeal, and alleviate my disbeliever's existential tension and the skeptic's mantra of, "show me." I inhaled and tried to adjust my body and ignore the muscular stresses.

My form in the mirror came in and out of focus. I tried to concentrate my eyes. But I caught my attention wandering and my eyes drifting. Janet sat ten feet away, and I glanced to her. Her red hair had darkened to the color of gunmetal. I watched her chest rise and fall, slow like a deep-sea swell, with each deep breath.

I reasserted myself and counted and let the air fill me, hold it and let it go. I stared into my darkened eye sockets until the rest of my body blurred to nothing. The minor aches and twitches died away. The temperature became nothing—neither hot nor cool. My mind blanked and tears filled the edges of my eyes from exertion, and I felt an inexplicable moment of silence: the cars on the street, the breathing of my partners and Paul's voice in his slow cadence disappeared, although later Carlos told me that Paul had never stopped. Even the sound of myself disappeared into a vacuum.

I had read in the *Hagakure: The Book of Hidden Leaves* that a samurai must lose himself, for his way is death. He must find that place which grants him peace with his non-existence, while accepting his temporary existence. It can be done through meditation. I didn't know if I had found that place, but I felt I had found something with each breath I no longer registered.

My attention started to draw toward the equipment room door to the right front of us. My temple tingled. It felt like I was being watched. As if something crouched in the shadow of the equipment locker. I wanted my moment of silence back, to lose my body in that small peace, but I had lost it. The strain returned to my thighs and my shoulders stiffened. I refocused on my darkened eyes in the mirror, as my neck muscles tensed, trying not to look to the corner.

I heard Paul's voice again, and started the count to clear my mind. I refocused on my breathing. My joints and lower back ached, but I pushed it out of my mind. I blinked my eyes, stared at the mirror, breathed. Again I wanted to look to the corner, almost as if someone gripped my head, trying to force me to look. I resisted and squinted, my eyes moist from effort of keeping them open. I inhaled a gold stream, my body relaxing, re-centering.

My lower back stiffened, and I arched it, shifting my hips to relax. I tensed my muscles, squeezing my buttocks and thighs as I took a breath and let it out. My reflection moved as I settled again, and stared at my face. Every time my concentration broke, I wondered if an apparition would materialize out of the darkness, a luminescent figure of an old Korean man in robes or the combat-fatigue-clad former instructor. I had no idea. I cleared my mind from the digression, focused and thought only of the breathing again—gold and smoke. Paul had also said our auras might become visible to us, if we relaxed and didn't look for it. We should see in the periphery of our vision a faint fluorescent glow of blue, red, yellow, orange, or some color outlining us like a halo of an ectoplasm aurora borealis. The shadow of my face's reflection was all I could see. I felt my attention drawn toward the locker room.

Janet screamed as something fell in the equipment locker, a thump and clatter of sticks. I jumped to Janet's side, as did Carlos. Paul and Daniel rushed for the equipment room door. She trembled and whimpered, but would not speak. Sweat beaded on her forehead and ran around her clenched eyes. Her breath caught in her throat and sounded like a flag popping in gusty winds. Finally, she said she had seen a man of light materialize in the corner by the equipment locker and walk toward her. She said, "It was like I was naked in front of a stranger."

I turned my head slowly and looked hard. I had to ask, "Is he still there?"

She shook her head and said, "He vaporized to nothing when I screamed." She pulled on my sleeve and whispered, "Nothing" again as if telling me a secret.

Everyone said they had felt their attention drawn to

the room, but no one had seen the man of light, only Janet. When she calmed down, I went over to the closet. Paul and Daniel snooped around the heavy kicking bags, gloves, pads, bamboo swords, staves, and assorted other things. They started to take things out and stacked them on the mat. I asked, "What fell?"

"A bag slid along the wall and hit those bo sticks and stuff. I mean a heavy bag too," Paul said.

I asked, "Sure it wasn't a mouse or something?"

Janet yelled, "I did not see a mouse!"

I nodded to her, and then walked past Paul and Daniel into the locker. I looked into the corners and along the baseboards. I ran my hands along the walls, feeling the coolness of the drywall and the slight rises in the bad taping job at the joints. I almost whispered, but some part of me felt foolish for having gone this far. I sensed nothing. No mice or signs of mice, no paranormal cold or hot spots, even as I stretched my arms the width of the small room, turning myself like an antenna searching for a faint signal, but picking up nothing but dead air.

Janet and I had come to humor Paul. She left converted to a world allowing for spirits, and in the same instant confirmed for herself the immortality of her own spirit. I wanted to believe with her, but I couldn't. How simple, I have often thought it would be to deny everything with the atheist's confidence, which is akin to faith, and requires a step outside of science. My life was governed by what I saw and experienced or was scientifically proved or explained in a well-wrought theory. These things go well with the world we hold and observe in common with others, but it does not mesh with the ineffable. Blaise Pascal said, "The heart has reason that reason knows not of," and St. Thomas Aquinas after a lifetime of contemplating nature as a means of understanding God, quit writing after an epiphany, saying his works were mere words "like so much straw compared to what I have seen and what has been revealed to me." Pascal and Aquinas believed Western reasoning and science could not illuminate the answer of afterlife and God. Perhaps they had tapped into some intuitive understanding of the human condition, the spiritual condition. I had never believed in sudden conversion or thought it possible someone could be struck with the light of faith. I believed they were politically motivated and said this to further the power and cause of their belief system without the certainty of science. But seeing Janet's face, I knew I had missed something and wished I had seen the ghost. Instead, I was left with neither proof nor disproof of ghosts or an afterlife. Many times since then, I have imagined the incandescent form, and then it dissolving like the light signature left in the aftermath of lightning.

Lightning and the man of light, the ghosts of fire lookouts, all types of charged air like the breath, charging me with life. The Taoists of ancient China believed each person had a predetermined amount of breaths he or she could take and developed exercises to slow their respiration to almost nothing—every measure of air delaying death by one long inhalation and exhalation at a time. I have faith in lightning, but not in ghosts. I know Janet saw something; her fear was as real as Ricochet's. I didn't know if they trembled in the presence of the mystical or if their fear was no more than being confronted with mortality, fearing the allure of the beautiful and luminous apparitions, which might drag them into the world of the undead. At least they believed in that possibility for what little comfort it brought them at the time.

I wanted to see a ghost out of my own existential terror. Confirm for me the unknown world others believe in as easily as they believe in lightning. I had learned martial arts to learn how to preserve my life and hone my perception in hopes of seeing the mystery. Then after all the training, Janet saw something. What was it that allowed her to see the mystery and me to remain in the dark? Is there no mystery, no grace and it was her mind in an altered state, deluding itself with the expectation fostered with autosuggestion or Paul's sincere suggestion? It is some beyond reason, like why one person survives a lightning strike and another doesn't, as in the case of Altmiller and Frazier a few feet apart on a lookout. I did not want to be alone in the field, waiting for the soles of my feet to be blown off. And now that I have two daughters I don't want to believe I brought them into a spiritless world.

Sometimes, when I am out on a wildfire that's dying down, and I lie out in the forest or on the high desert at night, I feel energy. It is the same energy I feel as a storm drives up a canyon or breaks hard over a ridge scattering lightning across the slopes. In both cases it was adrenaline, but it was mixed with an ineffable feeling of awe that is absent during other exciting moments, like when I am in a helicopter landing on a running fire. Unlike many people, I cannot equate those charged moments of strange wonder with spirits or the promise of the divine. If I saw a ghost, and believed, I could defend myself from the hideous depression—we drown in the rain of death and nothing persists. If I grasped some small part of the nature of ghosts or spirits, I would know that we might be less than lightning, but more than air.

FEVER AND GUTS

IV

I curl back into a ball and pass into blackness. My mind is in the crypt of consciousness. When I wake, the light in the room is the color of marble. My gut no longer aches, but is sore like I've been doing sit-ups all night. My body feels as if I've swum across the Aegean, and seawater has dried my skin. Soon hunger will gnaw my guts. Bleep bleep bleep. *Did you go to the hospital?*

No No matter what you have to eat, it takes guts. *Are you Okay?* Just living, going on day to day, takes guts. You stand the pain and go out alone in a fever, your skin wrapped in sheets that belong to someone else. Living in the dark dream of your past, episodic, uneven and mostly without sense. Bleep bleep bleep. *Are you Well?*

She is there, she still cares, but nothing will ever be the same no matter how I remember it. My daughters are there. They will never be ex-daughters. I hear music when they talk about horses and kites. But then there are tears. I have to go away again. To work. I tell them I am trying to make something better, but do not say I am failing at it. So many months away from them that, even when I go out for milk, their faces are braced for weeks. I call them, their voices as concrete as electric impulses. They talk of the last time I took them fly-fishing, the time we rode horses, and when we went to the symphony. Oh, Dad, and remember when we painted pottery? Papa, do you remember reading poems about me at the bookstore in front of the people? When I say yes, she asks if I can please do it again. I say yes, yes, to all they remember.

Their memories are out of order, but they make emotional sense. My last-wife says she is happy I am well and hopes I can come back soon to visit...we had some fun sometimes. I need a drink of water.

Let me know if you are well These memories of people are tidal, uncovering and covering and when you see any of them again, the tide will be high, concealing the absence and loneliness that seemed hard to live through—like the fever. God, can I just die right this very second? Eventually, it ends, as it must, and when it ends, I go on. When did the tide slip out again? It was high only a minute ago. Was it just yesterday I kissed that crooked smile, but of the first wife and not the last girlfriend? No, the big smile of my last-wife, the smile as bright as a lighthouse. No, the girlish smiles after a returning kiss on a blushing check. I sit up in bed. I rub my eyes and stretch, the fibrous ache from the dreams resilient. *Well, as well as can be*

All those others are gone past now, but their words were as real as raindrops falling into the sea. The fever still lies deep in my guts. My daughters smile from their school pictures on the wall. They are trapped in a riptide moment as they are trapped with the memory of when they last saw me—a snapshot of a younger me, a boat just out of reach on the current. They will have become women in that tide when all I will have is the memory of kids, floating on ocean swells, waving me back home.

Author Photo: Marie McLane

JERRY D. MATHES II is the author of the chapbook *Fall in the Borderland* and the poetry collection, *The Journal West*. His firefighting memoirs will be released from Caxton Press in 2013. Mathes has worked at South Pole Station, Antarctica, as a cargo specialist, and taught the southernmost poetry workshop in the world.

CPSIA information can be obtained at www.ICGtesting.com
Printed in the USA
LVOW131005181212

312205LV00001B/1/P